The
Book
of Why

The Book of Why

Robert L. Shook
illustrated by **Michael Senett**

HAMMOND®
INCORPORATED

MAPLEWOOD, NEW JERSEY   07040

Printed in the United States of America

Library of Congress Cataloging in Publication Data

Shook, Robert L., 1938-
    The book of why.

    Includes index.
    1. Questions and answers. I. Title.
AG195.S47   1983   031'.02   83-126
ISBN 0-8437-3335-7

To Nancy, Bruce, Jeff, Jon and Matt.
With my love.

PREFACE

Each of us has at one time or another asked, *Why*? In fact, some of the most ordinary occurrences in our lives deserve such a question. We encounter countless words, expressions, customs and superstitions every day that might puzzle us. Yet often we simply accept them without any curiosity as to how they began.

Many such questions have fascinating answers. There's often a very logical reason why things are the way they are. Other answers may reveal how illogical human customs and language can be. But whether the answer is logical or not, few of us can resist the opportunity to find out *why*, once the question is put before us.

It's amazing how many ordinary things we don't know. For example, while millions of us play the popular game of tennis, very few people know why the game is scored *15, 30, 40, game*. And for the golfers, why is a golf course called *the links?* Why does it have eighteen holes instead of a dozen or twenty?

I'll bet you twenty-five cents you don't know why we call a quarter *two bits,* or why we write from left to right. If it's a natural thing to do, why do the Hebrews write from right to left, and the Chinese from the top to the bottom of the page? And did you ever wonder why north is always at the top of a map? After all, the sun rises in the east. Why aren't maps oriented with east at the top? And why is time measured in *bells* aboard a ship? Why do we say people "put on the dog"?

So understanding *why* often helps to put things into their proper perspective. It's not always just a matter of collecting trivia for cocktail parties or for that once-in-a-lifetime opportunity to be a guest on a quiz show. Sure, it's fun to find out so many interesting facts, but it can also be useful.

So go ahead—enjoy yourself and learn *why*.

R.L.S.

Columbus, Ohio

"We are not amused!"

Why does royalty use "we" for "I"?

This custom may go back to the time when there were two Roman rulers in different cities who issued decrees jointly. The first English monarch known to use "the royal we" was Richard the Lionhearted. The custom survived in England until the twentieth century. The reasoning behind its use was that the ruler speaks for his subjects, not for himself alone. The use of the plural adds authority and dignity to his words. Editors and writers often use "we" so that their opinions appear impersonal. Using "we" also lets the writer avoid the frequent repetition of "I," which might appear egotistical.

Why is Chicago called "The Windy City"?

Although many tourists swear that Chicago winds are the worst anywhere, the city got its nickname because of its proverbially long-winded politicians, not its weather. In fact, despite Chicago's blustery reputation, it is not among the country's ten windiest cities, according to the National Climatic Center of the United States Weather Bureau, which ranks the leaders as follows:

	Average Wind Speed (mph)
1. Great Falls, Mont.	13.1
2. Oklahoma City, Okla.	13.0
3. Boston, Mass.	12.9
4. Cheyenne, Wyo.	12.8
5. Wichita, Kans.	12.7
6. Buffalo, N.Y.	12.4
7. Milwaukee, Wis.	11.8
8. Des Moines, Ia.	11.2
9. Providence, R.I.	10.9
Omaha, Nebr.	10.9
Dallas, Texas	10.9
Cleveland, Ohio	10.9

By comparison, Chicago is an oasis of calm, ranking sixteenth, with an average wind speed of only 10.4 miles per hour.

Why do we say "whipping boy"?

A "whipping boy" is a person who pays for someone else's mistakes—a scapegoat. This term dates back to a custom among European royalty. A prince would be raised and educated along with a commoner of the same age. And when the prince did something wrong, it was the commoner, his "whipping boy," who was punished.

Why do we say "Take it with a grain of salt"?

Since a Latin version of the phrase *cum grano salis* is familiar, it is sometimes assumed that the expression goes back to ancient Rome. The historian Pliny does use it in quoting an antidote for poison found in the palace of Mithridates. The antidote was to be taken on an empty stomach "plus a grain of salt." But this seems to be just a literal instruction. The phrase wasn't used to urge an attitude of skepticism until about three centuries ago. The idea behind it is that a meal is more palatable if salted. By extension, a listener can "swallow" a doubtful story more easily "with a grain of salt."

Why do we say "savvy"?

The noun "savvy" means understanding, general knowledge of affairs, or common sense. It comes from the Spanish *sabe,* a form of *saber,* meaning "to know." In Spanish, the letters *b* and *v* are pronounced very much alike and are sometimes interchangeable. Ranchers in the Southwest who picked up *sabe* heard it as a *v* rather than a *b* and pronounced and wrote it accordingly.

Why do we call it "pumpernickel bread"?

The German rye bread called "pumpernickel" was so named by Napoleon Bonaparte. He didn't particularly care for the bread, insisting that it was fit only for his horse, Nicole. As he expressed himself in French: *"pain pour Nicole."*

Why does the color red excite bulls?

It doesn't! The idea that red, especially if it's in motion, arouses a bull to fury is wrong. Bulls, like all cattle, are almost color blind. They can't tell the difference between red, pink, green, purple and white, as proven by experiments at the University of California. It is true that a bull's attention is attracted more easily by bright colors than by dull ones. But it is the general brightness of the bullfighter's costume and cape that attract the bull, rather than any specific color.

Why are knee-length pants called "knickers"?

It's a long way from the early "knickers" to the knee-length breeches that bear that name today. The first "knickers" (when New York was still New Amsterdam) were clay bricks. The man who baked them was, of course, the "knicker baker." Like many other occupational names (such as *Taylor* and *Mason*), Knicker-baker became a family name, sometimes changed to Knickerbocker. Since the name was so common among the Dutch settlers, Washington Irving used it as the name of the invented author of his book *A History of New York by Diedrich Knickerbocker.* Illustrations in the book showed the old Dutchmen wearing loose knee pants. Such breeches came to be called "knickerbockers," which was later shortened to "knickers."

Why do we say "out of the frying pan into the fire"?

Many languages use this expression or one that is similar. Italians say "from the frying pan into the coals," and the ancient Greeks said "out of the smoke into the flame." The Portuguese, Gaels,

and French also have similar expressions. Wherever it is used, the expression means stepping out of one bad situation into something worse.

Why do we say something "fits to a T"?

This phrase means to fit exactly. It is popularly thought that the "T" referred to is the draftsman's T square, which measures exact fit. But "to a T" was in use in the seventeenth century, before the T square got its name. A more likely explanation is that the expression was originally "to a tittle," which had much the same meaning. A tittle was the dot over the *i*, so the phrase meant "to a dot" or fine point. "Tittle" could easily have been shortened to "T," leaving us with the expression we have now.

Why are subversives called a "fifth column"?

This phrase, which became current in 1936, refers to people who secretly aid and abet the enemy. General Emilio Mola first used it during the Spanish Civil War. Leading four columns of rebels toward Madrid, he told newsmen he had a fifth column inside the city—an army of people who sympathized with him and would help his cause.

Why do we say "putting on the dog"?

In the 1870s, fashionable men wore high, stiff collars, military officers wore heavily braided collars, and women wore diamond chokers. College students referred to these collars as "dog collars." Since all three collars were worn on formal occasions, "putting on the dog" meant dressing in a style of pretentious splendor.

Why are oysters eaten only in the "R" months?

Nowadays oysters are offered on many menus the year round, and they can be eaten anytime. But many people still believe they should be eaten only in months that have the letter *R* in them. This idea precedes the time of modern refrigeration; it was difficult then to keep oysters alive during shipping in the heat of summer. Dead oysters spoil quickly, and not only smell bad but are poisonous. So the idea arose that oysters should be eaten only in the cooler months, which all happen to have the letter *R* in them.

Why is fish thought to be a brain food?

This notion became popular during the nineteenth century, when German scientists attempted to explain energy with the saying, "No phosphorus, no thought." They claimed this was the one element vital to the operation of the mind. The famous naturalist Louis Agassiz pointed out that fish are high in phosphorus, which would seem to make fish an ideal brain food. In fact, we now know that phosphorus is only one of many essential elements. "No calcium, no thought" is equally true. No one particular food nourishes the brain; what's good for the body is good for the mind.

Why does a drowning person surface three times?

He doesn't. This old idea is a myth, apparently based on the powerful mystic number *three,* the number of the Trinity. But there is no real evidence to support it. Drowning people may surface once or a dozen times, depending on how much water is in their lungs. Incidentally, in some primitive societies people are reluctant to rescue a drowning person, believing the water spirits will be angry if robbed of their prey.

Why does lightning never strike twice in the same place?

This belief stems from the ancient idea that the gods sent lightning for some specific purpose—often to punish someone or teach him a lesson. But once this had been done and the person survived, he and his property were forever safe from this sort of divine retribution. We now know that whatever draws lightning in the first place will draw it again and again. The Empire State Building and the Washington Monument, for instance, have each been struck numerous times, even several times during the same storm.

Why do we call the hottest part of summer "dog days"?

It was once thought that dog days were the time of year when dogs were more likely to become rabid. Actually, statistics show that most cases of rabies among dogs occur in early spring and late fall. This belief probably grew out of the phrase "dog days," rather than the other way around. It was the ancient Greeks and Romans who applied the name "dog days" to the period between July 3 and August 11, when the Dog Star, Sirius, rises at the same time as the sun. The ancients thought this conjunction was responsible for the heat and drought of midsummer.

Why is the fox believed to be cunning?

Actually, there is no evidence that the fox is more intelligent than any other animal. He does have two special characteristics, however, that may be the source of this belief. First, he is such an excellent runner that he often eludes pursuers. Also, he is a good actor. He will "play possum" until a group of geese approach within striking distance. Then the feathers fly!

Why do we believe chameleons change color to match their environment?

Unlike many superstitions, this one is rooted in fact. Chameleons do change color. But they do it only in response to marked changes in temperature and to their own emotions. Excitement or fear causes a sort of blushing mechanism to activate the yellow, red, green and black coloring matter just under the chameleon's transparent skin. It may happen that the change from, say, green to brown, will serve to blend the animal with his environment.

Why do card players call the pot "kitty"?

In many card games, players pool their winnings in a kitty. It is believed that the word "kitty" originates from the word "kit," which was commonly used to refer to a vessel, basket, bag, or other type of container. "Kit" was a common word as far back as 1400. Soldiers carried their money in a kit, which some believe is the origin of the term "kitty" used in card games.

Why isn't it always colder as you travel away from the equator?

It seems logical that the further a place is from the equator, the colder it will be. But prevailing winds, ocean currents, and mountains all affect temperature. Africa's glacier-topped Mt. Kenya, for instance, is only seven miles from the equator. There are places in Montana that reach temperatures 10 degrees colder than any ever recorded at the North Pole. And every summer at Fort Yukon, Alaska, the temperature soars above 90 degrees!

Why do we wait an hour after eating before going swimming?

Every child has been warned by his or her parents, "Don't go in the water until you have waited at least an hour, or you may get stomach cramps and drown." Some people believe digestion is slowed by exercising after a meal. Others think the chill of the water causes the blood to move to the surface, away from the digestive organs, thereby preventing digestion. And the fact that a person who is full usually doesn't feel like swimming also supports the idea that you shouldn't swim right after a meal.

While all these explanations sound reasonable, the belief that swimming after eating will cause stomach cramps is a myth. Many studies of athletes have shown that physical activity (such as swimming) after a meal does not cause stomach cramps or nausea. In fact, long-distance swimmers who swim twenty hours or more at a time are fed while they swim!

It is true that a beginning swimmer who fears the water may get a feeling of queasiness if he swims immediately after a meal. And since a competitive swimmer may have certain anxieties just before a race, he too may want to avoid eating. But these are strictly psychological effects. In itself, swimming right after a meal does not cause stomach cramps.

Why is the famous clock called "Big Ben"?

In fact, it isn't. Big Ben is the bell in the clock tower of London's Houses of Parliament that peals out the hour. This bell, which weighs thirteen tons, was named after Sir Benjamin Hall, Chief Commissioner of works at the time it was installed, because of his size.

Why do people believe night air is bad for you?

Thinking the disease that devastated Rome was carried on the wind from the fields around the city, the Romans named it *malaria,* or "bad air." It was not until 1898 that Italian scientists, following the lead of Charles Laveran, the French bacteriologist, proved that the disease was actually carried by the anopheles mosquitoes that infested Rome. Although it was now known that "bad air" did not cause the disease, it was true that the anopheles usually bites at night. Some took this to mean that night air is dangerous. This is still a widespread superstition. The fact is that there are no special infectious particles or vapors at night. Night air is generally cleaner, however, because there is less traffic—and therefore less dust.

Why do we think the heart is on the left?

The heart is actually in the middle of the chest. The origin of the popular myth is that the apex of the heart is a little to the left, so that it is easier to hear the heartbeat on that side.

Why do we believe people die or faint before hitting the ground in a fall from a great height?

This very common notion was fostered by writers and perhaps by early comic books, which invariably showed the pretty heroine fainting as she fell—only to be rescued by Superman, of course! It is true that a small minority of people would pass out from terror. But there is absolutely no reason to think someone who falls from, say, the Empire State Building, would be dead before reaching the ground. The fall itself is not fatal—it's the landing. Parachutists have free-fallen 7,000 feet and remained fully conscious and able to release their parachutes.

Why do people believe poison ivy is contagious?

The red, blistered rash caused by poison ivy looks much like that of measles, but it is not in fact contagious. However, bear in mind that the oils of the plant are what cause the irritation, and *they* may be passed from one person or animal to another. Interestingly enough, sensitivity to this plant is acquired—no one is born with it. In fact, only about half of the people who live in areas where it grows become sensitive to it.

Why do we say "turn the tables"?

When you "turn the tables" on someone, you reverse the situation and gain the upper hand. The idea derives from an old card game. A player who was at a disadvantage could turn the board around, giving the disadvantage to his opponent.

Why do we give children the father's surname?

Not all cultures trace lineage through the father's family. In Tahiti, for instance, children used to be named after the mother's side of the house. In Western culture the use of established surnames goes back to the time of Napoleon. Before that, a man had a given name and was known in addition as somebody's son. The Scandinavians expressed this with the suffix *son*, as in John*son*, or John's son. In Scotland a *Mac* or *Mc* before the name did the same thing: MacDonald was the son of Donald. In Ireland James, son of Neill, became James *O*'Neill. These names became fixed when Napoleon demanded that every man have a family name for record-keeping purposes—a patrynomic which all his descendents would bear.

Why do we say "fish in troubled waters"?

When you "fish in troubled waters" you are taking advantage of someone's mental upset to get something you want. This old expression grew from the fact, well-known among fishermen, that fish bite best in rough water.

Why do we believe that ostriches bury their heads in the sand?

The literary ostrich provides a very picturesque metaphor for somebody who is obviously blind to the true situation, and the commonly used expression "An ostrich with his head in the sand" has led many people to believe that ostriches really do bury their heads. The explanation given is that the ostrich thinks if *he* is unable to see his enemies, *they* are unable to see him. But the whole thing has no basis in fact. Like other animals, the ostrich flees when danger approaches. Although this myth has existed for a couple of thousand years, it is just that—a myth.

Why do women have one more rib than men?

They don't. Both sexes have twelve pairs of ribs. The basis for this belief is the story of creation as set forth in Genesis 2:21: ". . . and the rib, which the Lord God had taken from man, made he a woman." Some people think this implies that a woman has an extra rib. By the way, it *is* true that many women have one less "tail" vertebra than men.

Why do we think fat people are jolly?

This belief contradicts modern research, which has shown that many overweight people are unhappy. Indeed, many people overeat *because* they are unhappy. But obese people do *look* happier. Because of the extra fatty tissue under the skin, lines of strain tend not to show.

A related belief is that obese people are lazy. The truth is that their movements are often slowed by the extra weight they carry. This makes them look as though they are less active. But laziness—or very low energy, in other words—is caused by physical or psychological problems, which may affect anyone, fat or thin.

Why do people think Freud invented the term "id"?

It was Freud who gave this term its rich meaning as the wellspring of primal psychic energy. But he was merely adopting a term first used by a physician named Grodeck, *das Es. Es* is German for "it," although the meaning of the term was always more complex than that. When it came to translating from the German, however, "the it" was unsatisfactory, so the word was translated into Latin—which is *id*.

Why do we call a quarter "two bits"?

In England, the word *"bit"* has been applied to small coins for centuries. The British still use the term when they refer to a "threepenny bit." In the seventeenth and eighteenth centuries the Spanish *real* was equal to one eighth of a dollar. And in the West Indies the English colonists called the one *real* a "bit," and the two *real* "two bits." When the Spanish dollar was no longer in circulation, having been replaced by the United States dollar, there was no longer a twelve-and-a-half-cent piece that corresponded to the English shilling. Nevertheless, our twenty-five-cent coin, the quarter, is still referred to as "two bits."

Why is rice thrown at weddings?

This tradition is deeply rooted in ancient customs around the world. Some primitive peoples believed that jealous evil spirits attended weddings, hoping to injure the bridegroom. Rice was thrown to the spirits as a food, to distract them. The ancient Romans threw sweets and nuts at the bride, which later changed to confetti-throwing. The Saxons scattered a carpet of wheat and barley grains in the church for the bride to walk upon. These grains, like rice, symbolized prosperity and fruitfulness. The Orientals threw rice to bestow fertility upon the couple. In general, all grains and foodstuffs thrown at weddings were intended to bring good health and happiness to the newlyweds.

Why do we say a baseball player "bats .300"?

Actually, there is no logical reason. The meaning is the same, whether we say he "hits .300" or he "hits 30 percent of his times

at bat." Obviously, the percent system would not be nearly as impressive, so baseball statistics work on a base of 1,000.

Why do we say "put the screws on"?

The screws in this expression are thumbscrews, an old torture device. They were actually clamps that could be applied to a person's thumbs and gradually tightened with a screw. To "put the screws on" still means to apply pressure, but now in a figurative sense.

Why are daytime TV and radio serials called "soap operas"?

They're not musical, and they don't have anything to do with soap, but they're called "soap operas." The word *soap* comes from the fact that originally these melodramas were almost always sponsored by soap manufacturers. And the word *opera* is used in the same sense as in "horse opera," a common name for westerns. Although soap manufacturers aren't the only sponsors of today's daytime serials, the programs are still referred to as "soap operas" and probably always will be.

Why do we say "crocodile tears"?

Crocodile tears imply pretended grief. An old myth says that crocodiles moan and sigh like distressed people to lure passersby within reach of their jaws. Shakespeare made reference to crocodile tears in *Antony and Cleopatra, Othello* and *Henry VI.* While crocodiles have secretions in their eyes to keep them moist, they do not have tear glands. So, the truth is that crocodiles couldn't even weep if they wanted to.

Why do we call people who can perform abnormal digital gymnastics "double-jointed"?

The truth is, nobody has double joints. The people we call double-jointed are people who have very elastic ligaments, a trait that is usually inherited. Such people can do amazing acrobatics—but they aren't double-jointed.

Why is it impossible for a plane to hit an air pocket?

An air pocket is visualized as a sort of hole in the atmosphere, a place where there is no air. But such a thing is impossible. When a plane drops suddenly, what it has hit is properly called a downdraft. In fact, there are no airless pockets in the atmosphere.

Why is tennis scored fifteen, thirty, forty, game?

Originally, the game of tennis was scored: *fifteen, thirty, forty-five* and *game*. The *forty-five* was later shortened to *forty*. In the Middle Ages, sixty was regarded as a whole or round number, in much the same way as a hundred is today; there was, for instance, the association, from the thirteenth century onward, with the sixty minutes on a clock face. It took four points to win a game, so each was accorded a quarter of sixty, or fifteen. The six games for a set may well have come from multiplying six times sixty, or 360, the number of degrees in a complete circle; or, putting it the other way round, we can start with the circle of 360 degrees, divide it into six sixties (i.e., into six games), and divide each game, or sixty, into four points of fifteen each.

Why is north at the top of maps?

There's no scientific principle that makes this particular orientation essential. The ancient Greek and Roman maps placed east at the top because it was the direction of the rising sun. Medieval cartographers of Christian faith likewise chose east because they believed that the original Garden of Eden lay on the eastern borders of the known world. In the second century, for no reason in particular, the Greek geographer of Alexandria, Ptolemy, started the modern custom of placing north at the top of maps. During the Renaissance, Ptolemy's maps were accepted throughout Europe. Later, with the increased use of meridians and parallels in cartography, more and more maps were made with north at the top. Sailors' charts also used this orientation during the thirteenth century.

Why do we write from left to right?

If you think it's because it's the natural thing to do, then why do the Hebrews write from right to left, and the Chinese start their writing in the upper right-hand corner and run it down the edge of the sheet? It must be noted, however, that the majority of nations write from left to right, and that the right hand moves more easily toward its shoulder than away from it. This physical fact helps explain why left-handed people write in an awkward manner. With the left hand in front of the writing, the writer's vision is partially blocked unless the paper is slanted (or the wrist is bent on top of the written line). Also, the left hand will smear the wet ink as it moves along on top of the writing.

Why do some clock dials use "IIII" instead of "IV"?

When Roman numerals are used on clock dials, quite often "IIII" is used instead of "IV." Although there are many theories which explain this practice, most authorities believe that the original purpose was to make the IIII balance with the VIII on the opposite side.

Er, this is, er . . ."

Why is Independence Day celebrated on the fourth of July?

Almost everyone thinks the Declaration of Independence was signed on July 4. In fact, that's not what the document was called, and that's not when it was signed by all the members. The first of two documents involved was Richard Henry Lee's resolution on independence, passed by Congress on July 2. The next day two Pennsylvania newspapers printed the news that Congress had declared the colonies "free and independent states." The document we think of as the Declaration of Independence was the Report of the Committee of Five, drafted by Jefferson. This committee was appointed to prepare a statement explaining to the world why the colonies were taking this action. That report, officially titled "The Unanimous Declaration of the Thirteen United States of America," was amended and adopted on the fourth of July. On that day it was signed, not by all the members, but only by John Hancock on behalf of the Congress.

Why do we believe elephants never forget?

Superstition has it that an elephant's memory is so retentive that after years have passed it will remember a person who abused it and turn on that person. Elephants have been known to attack abusers, but never after a long period of time. In fact, elephants often fail to recognize their own keepers!

Why does a rabbit's foot mean good luck?

Since ancient times, the rabbit has been admired for its fertility. The foot was also considered a sacred part of the body because it came in contact with the earth, believed to be the source of life. The rabbit's agility and fertility were believed to be very pleasing to the gods. Therefore, the combination is thought to bring good luck to anyone carrying a rabbit's foot.

Why does a golf course have eighteen holes?

It could have ten holes or twenty, but why eighteen? In the early eighteenth century the golf course in St. Andrews, Scotland, had an even dozen holes. The course was not laid out in a roughly circular pattern with the last hole ending near the beginning, as today's courses are, but in a straight line. Since twelve holes weren't enough for a game, the player turned around at the last hole and worked his way back to where he began, thus playing twenty-two holes. Eventually the first four holes were made into two long ones, which reduced the round trip to eighteen holes. However, it wasn't until sometime later that the club made separate fairways and there were eighteen actual holes.

Why do golfers use tees?

Ever since the game of golf was invented in the late fourteenth century in Scotland, golf courses had tee boxes. These boxes contained sand and a pail of water; golfers would wet a little of the sand and make a tee. In 1920, however, Dr. William Lowell, a dentist from New Jersey who didn't like to get his hands messy, patented a little wooden peg which he called the "Reddy Tee." But his invention was not accepted until 1922. That year Walter Hagen, after winning the British Open, used the good doctor's tee in exhibitions all over the United States. He even carried one behind his ear. Such was his influence that that ended the sand-and-bucket days of golf.

Why do we observe St. Valentine's Day as we do?

There was nothing romantic about the story of the original St. Valentine. He was a Roman priest who helped rescue early Christian martyrs. For this he was put in jail and finally clubbed to death. But his day happened to fall on the same day as the feast of the birds, which celebrated the day on which birds were believed to pick their mates for the coming year. Because of the romantic association, Valentine's Day became the day when lovers exchange tokens of affection.

Why is a four-leaf clover considered good luck?

This very old superstition exists throughout Europe. One theory explaining its origin is that the shape of the clover resembles the shape of the cross. The idea that a four-leaf clover brings luck, however, is older than Christianity. Evidence of this is the belief in some countries that in order for the charm to work, the clover must be picked on Midsummer Eve. This suggests that the charm goes back to primitive sun worshipers, who at the summer solstice gathered plants thought to have magic powers. Priests may have attached special significance to these relatively rare plants. There is no species of clover that is four-leaved, by the way. All types will occasionally produce such plants; white clover—the kind often found in lawns—tends to produce the most.

Why is seven considered a lucky number?

To understand this ancient superstition, we have to imagine the numbers as shapes, the way the ancients did. Four was made by tallying four lines, as in a cross, which represented the human body. So did the square, also composed of four lines. The number three was a triangle and symbolized the spiritual, the trinity of Mother, Father, and Son in which primitive peoples believed. When three and four were put together, the result was a square topped by a triangle, and the number was represented by the figure ⌂ .

This was seen as man's complete house—body below and spirit above. Thus, seven was a powerful and lucky number. One of many superstitions associated with this number was that the seventh son of a seventh son would rise to greatness.

Why do people think a black cat is unlucky?

Cat superstitions started in Egypt, where the cat was a sacred emblem of the cat-headed goddess Pasht. We owe the idea that cats have nine lives to the Egyptians, for Pasht had nine lives. Black cats were especially revered, and were mummified and buried in special graveyards. Later, people believed cats were the consorts of witches. These witches, they thought, always boiled the brain of a black cat in their potions. It was through this association that the black cat came to be considered a sign of bad luck.

Why do we believe breaking a mirror will bring seven years of bad luck?

This superstition began with the Romans, who believed life renewed itself every seven years. Since a mirror held a person's image, when it was broken the health of the breaker—the last person to look into it—was also broken. It would not mend until seven years had passed. A rather different ancient superstition was that the gods broke a mirror to prevent a person from seeing a tragic event that was about to happen in his life. This led to the idea that breaking a mirror foretold a death in the family. These superstitions persisted because mirrors were very expensive. The servant in a wealthy house who broke one was indeed in for some bad luck.

Why do we celebrate April Fool's Day?

Festivals of this sort go back at least to ancient Rome, where the Feast of Fools was celebrated on February 17. Hindus also have a time consecrated to making practical jokes—the Huli Festival—which takes place in early spring. The English apparently borrowed from France the custom of tricking people on April 1. There, the April fool, or person the joke is played upon, is called *un poisson d'avril*—an April fish. This may refer to the fact that a young April fish would be easily tricked by a lure. April 1 was not set as All Fool's Day until after the Gregorian calendar was instituted. Under the old Julian calendar, in which March was the first month, the New Year was celebrated with an eight-day festival beginning March 25. April 1 was the peak, devoted to bringing gifts to friends and neighbors. After the Gregorian calendar was adopted in 1752, New Year's Day became January 1. But some people, as practical jokes, still gave gifts on April 1. This is the most likely explanation for the origin of April Fool's Day.

Why do we make New Year's resolutions?

The ancient Romans believed January was ruled by the god Janus, who had two faces, one looking back on the past year, and one looking ahead toward the new. To ensure a good year, they honored him with sacrifices and good conduct during his month. Our own present-day custom of resolving to change for the better on New Year's Day comes down from them.

Why is National Election Day on the Tuesday after the first Monday in November?

Until 1845, each state could choose the date for holding its national election, as long as that date was no more than 34 days before the first Wednesday in December, the fixed time for the meeting of electors. While all the states elected in November, the varying dates made repeat voting too easy. In choosing a uniform day, Congress wanted the election to be held about thirty days before the electoral meeting. A number of states had previously met on Monday or Tuesday. For practical reasons, the legislators thought it best to have one day between Sunday and Election Day. They considered the first Tuesday, but thought it would be inconvenient for businessmen if it should fall on the first of the month. The second Tuesday could fall as late as the 14th, leaving only 22 days until the meeting of the electors. The first Tuesday after the first Monday, however, would never fall later than November 8, and would always be about 30 days before the meeting of the electors.

Since then, the time of the meeting of electors has been changed twice, but the date of national Election Day is still the same.

Why do we teach children that Santa Claus brings gifts on Christmas?

Santa is a direct descendent of the venerated St. Nicholas. A pious young man, he decided to give away the money he inherited from his parents. He heard of a man in town who was considering selling his three daughters into slavery because he had no dowries for them. One night Nicholas secretly dropped a bag of gold inside the man's window, and soon after the oldest daughter married. Nicholas repeated the act twice more, but on the third night the man, curious to know who his benefactor was, caught him. Nicholas swore him to secrecy.

Because of his generosity and the many miracles he worked, Nicholas was canonized. He is the patron saint of Russia and Greece. Europe has always honored December 6, the day of his death, as St. Nicholas Day, and that was the day of gift-giving, because Nicholas is also the patron saint of children. In some countries he is seen as carrying a bag of presents for good children and birch rods for bad ones. The name "Santa Claus" is, of course, a corruption of Saint Nicholas. It was Washington Irving who first described him as a jolly fellow flying through the air in a reindeer sleigh. The famous political cartoonist Thomas Nast gave him his red fur-trimmed suit.

Why do we believe in three square meals a day?

The only reason for this habit is custom. Perhaps it's most convenient to eat before work, during one work break, and after arriving home. But studies suggest that those "three squares" are too few. Between meals the fuel continues to burn. Five small meals a day would keep the metabolism running along at a more even rate.

Why is Mardi Gras celebrated in New Orleans?

Mardi Gras, originally a Catholic celebration, falls on the day before Lent, Shrove Tuesday. On this day *shrift,* or confession, was made to prepare the soul for Lent. *Mardi Gras* itself is a French term meaning "fat Tuesday." On this day it was the custom in France to parade a fattened ox through the streets of the city. Since Lent was a period of fasting, Mardi Gras was the last chance for feasting and general revelry. Many Catholic cities in Europe still hold carnivals on this day. The New Orleans pageant was started by the area's French settlers, and reached its present form around the middle of the nineteenth century.

Why is there an Easter Bunny?

The Easter Bunny himself was probably a creation of candymakers, who depicted him carrying baskets of sweets to children. But he has roots in a long tradition. Easter is related to the sun worshipers' rites of spring. Because of his fecundity, the hare symbolized to them the renewed fertility of earth and the abundant life the returning sun brings. In Egypt the date of Easter is set by the moon's orbit, and rabbits, because they are born with their eyes open, are connected to the "open-eyed moon" of Easter. The word "Easter" comes from a Norse goddess, Eastre or Ostara. Germans believed the hare was her sacred animal, and that it laid eggs for good children on Easter Eve.

Why do we celebrate Christmas on December 25?

Actually, there is no evidence that this was Christ's birthday. And many people have noted that December 25 falls during the rainy season in the Holy Land—shepherds would probably not be out in their fields. The date was most likely chosen because it is close to the winter solstice, a time of many pagan festivals. In the early days of Christianity many different dates were used, and December 25 was not officially adopted until 354. Still, not all Christians celebrate Christ's birth on that day. The Eastern Orthodox and Ukrainian Catholic churches, who go by the old Julian calendar, celebrate Christmas thirteen days later.

Why do we kiss under the mistletoe?

This custom derives from an ancient Scandinavian myth. Freya, goddess of love, invoked a charm that her son Balder might be protected against anything which came out of the four elements—earth, air, fire, or water. But the god of evil and jealousy, Loki, created a dart out of mistletoe. Because the plant is a parasite which grows on trees and does not come from elements, the dart pierced Balder's heart and killed him. Freya wept bitterly. But as her tears turned to pearls and fell on the mistletoe, the gods brought Balder back to life. Freya decreed that the mistletoe would thereafter be an instrument only for good. Since she presides over love and marriage, it is said that lovers who kiss under the mistletoe can never be harmed.

Why are prisoners executed just before dawn?

Carrying out executions in the early morning is an ancient practice. It may date back to the prehistoric sun worshipers, who made sacrifices at dawn. On the other hand, it has long been a military practice to shoot condemned men as soon as it is light enough for the firing squad to see. At present, the court sets the date of the execution and the time is up to the prison officials. An execution upsets inmates, and early morning is usually chosen because they are still in their cells and asleep.

Why are engagement rings worn on the fourth finger?

This custom goes back at least to second-century Egypt, where it was believed that a delicate nerve connected the fourth finger of the left hand with the heart. In the Middle Ages the connection was thought to be a blood vessel, sometimes called the *vena amoris* —love's vein.

Why do women wear wedding rings?

This custom did not originate as a symbol of bondage to the husband—just the opposite. In biblical times it was the custom for a man to wear a signet ring, which he might give to an agent as a symbol of his authority. Whoever carried his ring could act in the man's name. In time it became the practice for the man simply to stamp authorization papers with the seal on his ring. When the Egyptian woman was given her husband's ring, she was trusted to issue commands in his name, so it meant that the marriage was a full partnership.

Why are old shoes tied to the back of newlyweds' cars?

This tradition comes from a number of sources. Shoes have often been linked with fertility, as in China, where a shoe from the shrine of the Mother Goddess can make a childless woman fertile. Another reason for the shoe tradition in many countries is that leather is thought to keep evil spirits away. Shoes have also been used to signify ownership. Among the Hebrews a sandal changed hands to signify the closing of a contract for a purchase of land. And an Anglo-Saxon father would give the bride's shoe to her husband, who would then demonstrate his new authority over the bride by touching her on the head with it!

Why do brides wear veils?

This custom comes from several sources. One is the Muslim practice of Purdah, which forbade a man to see his financée's face until the wedding. All unmarried women were secluded and kept entirely covered. After the ceremony the groom lifted the veil and exclaimed at his bride's beauty. The veil may also be a relic of the canopy held over the couple's head in many ancient ceremonies. Such canopies are still used today in Jewish weddings. Both canopies and veils have often been used to protect the bride from the "evil eye" of anybody who might wish her ill.

Why does the wedding ceremony end with a kiss?

Today, as part of the wedding ceremony, the groom kisses the bride—a symbolic seal of the vows of matrimony. This was not always so. In ancient times the kiss was used only as a gesture of respect for a ruler. Natives in some African tribes still kiss the ground the chief has walked on. Early Romans kissed the eyes in greeting. And one Roman emperor let his favored courtiers kiss his lips; less-favored nobles could kiss his hands, and those with the least status had to kiss his feet! So the kiss as a form of homage has always been common. But the kiss between man and woman is a more recent custom than we think. It was in France that the kiss first became accepted in courtship. It quickly became so popular that every dance ended with a kiss. As affectionate kissing became customary, the betrothal kiss, a sign of good faith, was added to the wedding ceremony. To us, kissing seems natural, but in fact the affectionate kiss is unknown among most primitive peoples.

Why do we say "cut off your nose to spite your face"?

This expression originated in 1593, when Henry IV was King of France, and the Parisians were making it abundantly clear that they did not want him as their king. Outraged, Henry declared war on his beautiful capital city and surrounded it with cannons. At which point one of his men found the courage to ask: "What good is it to be king of a dead city? Wouldn't that be like cutting off your nose to spite your face?"

However much this striking figure of speech had to do with it, Henry did spare the city, and went on to become one of France's most beloved monarchs.

Why do men's coat sleeves have buttons?

While the buttons on men's coats are a matter of style and custom, there are two theories about their origin. The practical explanation is that the buttons held back the sleeves and freed the hands in earlier times when sleeves were much longer than our present styles. However, according to legend, Frederick the Great of Prussia objected to his soldiers wiping their faces with their coat sleeves. With buttons on the sleeves of his uniform, a soldier would scratch his face whenever he attempted to wipe his brow or nose.

Why is walking under a ladder considered unlucky?

Many people refuse to walk under a ladder that is leaning against a building, for fear that it will bring bad luck. If they must do it, they cross their fingers as a countercharm. There are several traditional reasons for this taboo. One was derived from early paintings of the Crucifixion, which showed a ladder leaning against the Cross. Satan stood beneath the ladder gnashing his teeth, frustrated by Christ's dying to save humanity. The space under ladders became associated with Satan, dangerous territory. In Asiatic countries the superstition came from the custom of hanging criminals from the rung of a ladder propped against a tree. The ghost of the victim was thought to loiter around the ladder indefinitely, shocked by the sudden death. Anyone who met the ghost might die—since death was at that time thought to be contagious. Finally, in France it was at one time customary to force a criminal to walk under the ladder to the gibbet (a sort of gallows) before he climbed it. In England the superstition is specific; an unmarried woman who walks under a ladder will remain single for a year.

Why do we cross our fingers against bad luck?

To express hope that nothing will interfere with our plans, we may cross our fingers. This ancient superstition really represents making the sign of the cross. The cross was seen as the symbol of perfect unity. Since the wish was held where the two lines meet, it could not slip away before it came true. Originally, wishes were made by one person placing his index finger on top of the index finger of another to form a cross. One made the wish and the other supported it. In time this changed so that the powerful cross could be made by one alone. An interesting version of this is the children's superstition that a lie doesn't count if you cross your fingers while telling it. The reasoning is that one is punished for lying; but crossed fingers will prevent that bad luck. And if one is *not* punished, he has not really told a lie at all. The lie doesn't count.

Why are there so many superstitions regarding left-handedness?

In most languages, the words for "left-handed" also mean "insincere" or "treacherous." Our own word "sinister" is Latin for "left." The Romans thought that the left side, which they thought was ruled by the heart, was dangerous. Since the heart represented emotion, the heart side had to be carefully watched. Many primitive peoples have distrusted left-handed people simply because they were in a minority.

Why do we believe that opening an umbrella indoors brings bad luck?

Early umbrellas did not open as easily as they generally do today. The stiff, clumsy spring that operated them thrust the umbrella open in a sudden and dangerous fashion. If this was done indoors, it was almost sure to damage something or hurt someone. Such an accident might also bring on an argument—enough bad luck to start a superstition!

Why do we speak of getting up on the wrong side of the bed?

There is an ancient taboo against getting out of bed on the left side. The Romans feared the left, or *sinister,* side, as that was where evil demons lurked. A second superstition says that whichever side of the bed you get in on is the side you should get out on. Otherwise, you have interrupted the "circle" and will have a bad day. If you do get up on the wrong side of the bed, you can prevent bad fortune by walking backwards to the bed and starting all over again.

Why were duels always held at dawn?

In every swashbuckling movie, duels take place in the morning mist. The reason for this custom was the correct belief that an abdominal wound is far more difficult to treat if the victim has recently eaten. So the real point of meeting at dawn was that both men's stomachs were empty.

Why do paratroopers yell "Geronimo"?

One theory has it that this custom began at Fort Sill, Oklahoma, where there was a series of steep hills. It is said there that one day, being hotly pursued by the army, Geronimo made a horseback leap down an almost vertical cliff into water. The army did not dare to follow him. In mid-leap he cried out, "Geronimo!" The story hung on, and the idea of shouting "Geronimo!" was picked up by paratroopers training at Fort Bragg and Fort Campbell. Paratroopers yell for a good reason. It's necessary for them to breathe deeply during a jump, and taking in breath to shout reminds them to do that.

Why do we cover our mouths when we yawn?

Early peoples feared that when they yawned, all the breath would

escape from their bodies and they would die. Others believed an evil spirit might enter the open mouth and cause illness or death. So covering the mouth when you yawn did not begin as a point of etiquette, but as self-protection.

Why is "SOS" used as a distress signal?

What do these letters stand for? Some say "Save Our Souls"; others, "Save Our Ship." Actually, the letters are an arbitrary signal. The original telegraph distress signal was "CQD." "CQ" was the general alert that a message would follow, and "D" stood for "distress." But for technical reasons this signal didn't work well. It was decided that a signal of three dits, three dahs, and three dits would be easy to send and understand. It was simply a coincidence that this translated to "SOS."

Why is thumbs down a gesture of rejection?

Many people think thumbs down was the gesture used by the ancient Romans to signify that a gladiator should be killed. Evidence indicates, however, that just the opposite was true: thumbs *up* meant death, and thumbs *down* was a request to drop the sword. It was a nineteenth-century French painter, Jean Léon Gérôme, who reversed the gestures in his "Pollice Verso" in 1873. The picture shows spectators, thumbs pointing down, demanding that a gladiator be put to death. This often-reproduced picture led to the general notion that thumbs down was a negative gesture.

Why do we believe a common cold comes from cold weather?

This is strictly an ancient belief. It is true that getting chilled does lower resistance; but colds are caused by a virus, not by cold weather. In *cool* weather, however, we are most susceptible to colds; thus, colds are most frequent in the fall and least frequent in

June and July. It's interesting to note that the coldest months, December through February, are not the months when the chance of catching a cold is greatest. In fact, Eskimos rarely caught colds until the virus was introduced by arctic explorers.

Why do people think cats have nine lives?

In ancient Egypt there was a traditional belief that cats had rid the land of a plague of rats. For this reason the cat was worshiped and associated with the trinity of Mother, Father, and Son. To figure out how many extra lives the cat had, the Egyptians multiplied the sacred number three times itself and arrived at nine. Their belief in the cat's extraordinary qualities was enhanced by their observation that it nearly always lands on its feet. It is in fact the flexibility of the cat's spine, and not anything supernatural, that gives it this ability.

Why is three on a match bad luck?

At one time it really was. This superstition is said to have arisen during World War I. If soldiers in the trenches kept a match lit long enough to light three cigarettes, the enemy would have time to aim—so the thinking went. A match that was extinguished quickly was less dangerous. During World War II the match shortage was so acute that everyone was urged to share lights, and "three on a match" came to be taken less seriously.

Why do we knock on wood?

This superstition survives today as a way of warding off bad luck after bragging or talking of good luck. One possible origin of this belief in the magical power of wood is the ancient game of "wood tag," in which the player who manages to touch wood cannot be captured. Knocking on wood might also date back to the time of primitive tree worship, when knocking on a tree was thought to summon up the friendly spirit who lived in it.

Why is the owl considered wise?

The Greek goddess Athena, who ruled the intellectual side of life, was probably first worshiped in the form of an owl. Later, as she assumed human form, the Greeks came to regard the owl as her favorite bird. One of the curious things about the owl is that its eyes cannot move in the sockets; it must turn its flexible neck in order to look to the side. This, combined with its nocturnal nature and distinctive call, make it an easy subject for superstition.

Why is it said that storks bring babies?

This superstition evolved out of the belief that the stork brings good luck. Since the stork was sacred to Venus, goddess of love in Roman mythology, ancient Romans believed that if storks nested on a roof it was a sign of her blessing upon the household. In Norse legend the bird flew around the Cross at the Crucifixion, crying to Jesus, *"Stryka"* (strengthen). Perhaps because of these legends, the stork was welcome as the guardian of German and Dutch homes. It was said that a stork would fly over the house just before a birth, announcing the family's good luck. Parents who had trouble explaining where babies came from found it natural to point to the beautiful white bird on the house.

Why should a sleepwalker not be awakened suddenly?

In old Harold Lloyd cliffhangers, sleepwalkers might walk on girders a hundred stories up and never miss a step—as long as they weren't awakened. But if awakened, they would be so terrified they would fall. Actually, there are no recorded cases of sleepwalkers getting themselves into positions of such great danger. It is true that a sleepwalker who is awakened may be confused as to what was dream and what is reality. But the confusion will probably pass very quickly. The idea that it won't can be traced back to the belief of many primitive peoples that during sleep the soul travels, and a person must be awakened gradually so that it has time to return.

Why is the number thirteen considered unlucky?

The human habit of giving magical powers to numbers is very old. Seven is a lucky number, for instance. We find it again and again in the Bible, from the seven days of creation to the seven golden candlesticks of Revelation. So strong is the power of this ancient habit of mind, that if a group of people are asked to write down any number below ten, seven will be the number most often chosen. The association of bad luck with thirteen dates to the time of Christ. Thirteen people attended the last supper on the eve of the Crucifixion. Even today some people shy away from sitting at a table with twelve others, in the belief that thirteen at table means that one of them will soon die.

Why do we give the "evil eye" to a person we don't like?

While today the evil eye is merely a hostile look, ancient superstition held that the evil eye could harm or even kill. There are many expressions involving the way we look at somebody, such as "looking daggers," "dirty looks," "if looks could kill," and "the Indian sign." These arise from the widespread ancient belief that witches had the power of the evil eye. In Rome, a professional witch could actually be hired to bring harm to one's enemies. Gypsies, who themselves were thought to have the evil eye, spread belief in such power throughout Europe and Asia. Medieval people were so convinced of these powers that anyone with a peculiar cast in his eye was liable to be burned at the stake as a witch. The bridal veil originated as a protection against the evil eye.

The word "pupil" (of the eye) is derived from the Latin word *pupilla,* which means "little doll." Undoubtedly, early people were fascinated to see their own images in miniature in the eyes of others; they believed that they would be in great personal danger if their likeness should lodge permanently in an evil eye. In more modern times superstitious people have believed that the murderer's image will remain in the eye of his victim.

Why do we use a "V" to symbolize victory?

In modern times this symbol was popularized by Belgian students during World War II. Forming a Freedom Movement, they escaped to England to join the Belgian Army there. The Flemish word for freedom, *vrzleid,* was their identification sign, and its first letter was signified by the parted index middle fingers. Those who reached England introduced the symbol there, and it rapidly spread throughout the Allied forces.

The "V" symbol is actually quite ancient, however. The Egyptians wore amulets showing the forked fingers of the god Horus, who symbolized the victory of good over evil. At one time "V" and "U" were interchangeable, and since both symbolized the crotch of the human body, they were symbols for life itself and its continuation.

Why do people rub frostbite with snow?

This old belief may be due to the expression "a blanket of snow," or to the idea that birds and small creatures stay warm beneath a covering of snow. The arctic explorer Vilhjalmur Stefansson, who lived for two years with the Eskimos, said he knew of many explorers who had frozen their whole faces by rubbing them with snow. All you have to do when frostbite threatens your face, he said, is to press your hand, warm from your mitten, on the cold spot. Warmth, not cold, combats frostbite.

Why do we believe a Horatio Alger hero always ended up wealthy?

We usually speak of "a Horatio Alger story" in reference to a person who goes from poverty to great wealth. Actually, none of Alger's heroes became really wealthy. They were honest newsboys and bootblacks who worked hard and eventually became respectable. But their successes were modest, as were their expectations. A raise from $5 to $10 a week gave the book a happy ending.

Why are cows milked from the right side?

A cow can be trained to be milked from either side. Whatever side she is trained on, the animal will usually resent being milked from the other, and may not cooperate. For this reason it is convenient to train all cows to one side. The reason the right side is preferred over the left is that most people are right-handed and prefer to milk with their stronger hand. When the milker sits on the right side of the cow, his right arm has more room to maneuver.

Why do we have cornerstone ceremonies?

Our primitive ancestors believed in a powerful earth god who might become angry if his territory was violated. When any building was erected, this god was appeased by the offering of a human sacrifice. Later the sacrifice was a sheep or bullock, always offered by the shaman or magician. In some places the human or animal victim was buried in the walls, and bones have been found in many ancient dwellings. Today only a scroll or some other substitute is placed in the cornerstone, and the officiating person is not a shaman but a dignitary.

Why are three golden balls the sign for pawnbrokers?

The Medici family of Florence originated the use of this symbol. Legend has it that Averardo de Medici, an officer under Charlemagne, killed a giant whose war club was decorated with three gilded balls. To commemorate this feat, Averardo adopted the three golden balls as a family symbol. Since the family was at that time prominent in medicine, the golden balls, which were interpreted as pills, came to represent the entire medical profession. After the Medici family turned to banking and pawnbroking, the device gradually came to stand for the pawnbroker's trade.

Why do we fly the flag at half mast as a sign of mourning?

As the word "mast" indicates, this custom originated at sea, where ships would lower their flags to signal surrender. Half-masting a flag is also a sign of distress. Proper flag etiquette in this situation is to raise the flag to the top of the staff and slowly lower it to the middle.

Why are men's lapels notched?

This style goes back to the time when all men wore coats with military collars. Outdoors these collars were buttoned high; indoors they were unbuttoned, and in warm weather the front of the jacket was rolled back. It became popular to wear jackets open and rolled back, and this style became the lapeled jacket of today. The notch is the point where originally the jacket and collar joined.

Why do men lift their hats to women?

The custom of uncovering the head to greet somebody seems to go back to ancient military practices. When an armored knight removed his protective helmet, it expressed his confidence in the person he was greeting. This grew into the custom of removing the hat as a sign of respect for a superior. That this should in time become a way of showing gallantry to women is not surprising. Men still remove their hats as a gesture of respect when saluting the flag.

Why do we say "All that glitters is not gold"?

This aphorism is found in various forms throughout Continental literature. In the twelfth century, Alain de Lille wrote: "Do not hold everything gold that shines like gold." Both Chaucer and Shakespeare used versions of the saying. Cervantes, in *Don Quixote,* put these words in the mouth of Sancho Panza: " 'Tis an old saying, the Devil lurks behind the cross. All is not gold that glisters." But the first occurrence in its present form is in John Dryden's poem "The Hind and the Panther," published in 1687. The line in question reads: "All, as they say, that glitters is not gold."

Why is the word "bedlam" used to describe confusion?

"Bedlam" today means simply noise and confusion. Actually, it is a contraction of a place name—*Bethlehem,* an insane asylum in London. Centuries ago a visit to Bedlam was a popular amusement. People paid to stroll the corridors and watch the patients, who were safely behind bars. It was much like visiting a zoo, except that it was customary to make fun of the inmates and try to provoke them. The halls of such a place on visiting days must indeed have been bedlam.

Why do we say "behind the eight ball"?

To be "behind the eight ball" is to be in an unfavorable position. The phrase comes from a popular version of pool. The player has to sink the balls in numerical order, except for the black ball, number eight, which is sunk last. A player is penalized if he hits the eight ball, and loses the game if he sinks it out of turn. So a ball that lies directly behind the eight ball is in a bad position.

Why do we use "V" for "U" in inscriptions?

This practice began because there is no *U* in the Latin alphabet. The earliest *U* was merely the script form of *V*. This is why *W* is called "double-U," although it is really two *V*'s. It was not until about 1800 that English dictionaries gave the letters different positions. But *V* continued to be used because it lends itself to the sculptor's chisel. Incidentally, when *V* is used for *U* this way, it's known as the "manuscript U."

Why are red, white, and blue the colors of the United States flag?

Schoolbooks credit Betsy Ross with designing the flag, but historians believe this is not true. While a committee of three was appointed by Congress for this purpose, it is not known which member suggested the design that was used. George Washington, who was on the committee, did suggest a partial interpretation: "We take the stars from heaven, the red from our mother country, separating it by white stripes, thus showing that we have separated from her; and white stripes shall go down to posterity representing liberty."

Why do we bless sneezers?

The habit of blessing sneezers is both worldwide and ancient. When anyone in his presence sneezed, the Roman Emperor Tiberius would say, *"Absit omen"* ("May any bad omen be absent"). In New Zealand a charm was said to prevent misfortune when a child sneezed. DeSoto's band, exploring the New World, was amazed to find that the Indians chanted a blessing at a sneeze, just as they spoke one. Some authorities say that all such habits go back to the primitive belief that demons can enter the body through the open mouth. Thus, every sneeze puts you in danger and must be blessed. Our own use of such phrases as *"Gesundheit"* and "God bless you!" goes back to the Middle Ages. During the Plague

years, a sneeze was regarded as a sign that a person had the plague, in which case divine aid was sorely needed. The word *Gesundheit* is the German word for "health," and is also used as a toast.

Why do we say a poor person is "down on his uppers"?

If a person is "down on his uppers," he is flat broke. He has worn right through the soles of his shoes and is virtually barefoot, with only the uppers left to protect his feet.

Why do we have barber poles?

The barber pole with its spiral stripes indicates that at one time barbers were surgeons. Records show that as early as A.D. 500, barbers extracted teeth, treated wounds, and bled patients. During the reign of England's Henry VII, Parliament passed a law stipulating that barbers confine themselves to minor operations, such as bloodletting and drawing teeth, and prohibiting surgeons from cutting hair and shaving their patrons. The barber pole was the emblem of the barber-surgeon profession; and, because most people could not read in those days, the poles enabled them to recognize a barber shop. The white represents the bandage used in bloodletting, and the red stripe represents blood.

Why is the Gideon Bible in hotel and motel rooms?

The Gideon Society (the Christian Commercial Travelers Association of America), according to its declaration, was organized for the purpose of banding together Christian travelers to prepare their hearts for salvation. Hence, they supply Bibles to hotels and motels. The society was organized on July 1, 1899, in Janesville, Wisconsin, by three commercial traveling men—S. E. Hill, W. J.

Knights and John H. Nicholson. The name "Gideon," one of Israel's judges (from Judges 6 and 7), was chosen to honor his three hundred followers who overthrew the Midianites. Funds for purchasing the Bibles are raised by members of local churches throughout the country.

Why are the days of the week so named?

For much of history there was no week—calendars were simply arranged around lunar months. Our week derives from the fact that the Babylonians held market days every seventh day. The Jews copied this custom and added the Sabbath, also observed every seventh day. It was the Jews who first named the week, using numbers, with Saturday, the Sabbath, as day seven. The Romans adopted the seven-day week and named it after the Egyptian system—one day for the sun, one for the moon, and one for each of the five known planets. The names we use were derived from the Anglo-Saxons, who patterned their names on those of the Romans. Thus the day of the sun became *Sunnandaeg* (Sunday). The day of the moon was *Monandaeg* (Monday). Tuesday was *Tiwesdaeg,* after Tiw, their god of war. The next day had been named after Mercury, but the Anglo-Saxons called it after the god Woden (Wednesday). Jupiter, the thunderer, became Thor, the thunder god (Thursday). The next day honored Frigg or Freya, wife of Odin (Friday). The day of Saturn was *Saeternsdaeg* (Saturday). Incidentally, at one time a day was counted as the space between sunrise and sunset. It was the Romans who conceived of a day as running from midnight to midnight, the method now used.

Why do illiterates sign their names with "X"s?

This "X" is actually a St. Andrew's Cross. During the Middle Ages everyone, whether he could write his name or not, put a cross on any document he signed. This was a pledge by his Christian faith that he was sincere. The "X"s that represent kisses at the close of a letter are also crosses. They became associated with kisses because, as an act of reverence, signers often kissed the crosses they put at the bottom of documents.

Why is it called a "Teddy bear"?

Toy bears became popular in Germany around the turn of the century. In the fall of 1902 they were imported into the United States. At about that time President Teddy Roosevelt went on a hunting trip in Mississippi. It was reported that he refused to shoot a small bear which was brought into his camp for that purpose. Cartoonist Clifford Berryman was inspired by this and drew a cartoon of the incident, labeling it "Drawing the Line in Mississippi." The public, highly amused by the whole thing, began to associate the popular toy bears with Teddy's hunting adventures, and the phrase "Teddy bear" became nationally known.

Why is time indicated at sea by bells?

Before clocks were invented, the ship's bell was struck when the half-hour sandglass was turned over, thereby notifying the sailors on deck of the time of day. The term "bells" is still used today. The American Navy has six watches during a twenty-four-hour period, with the first shift beginning at 8 P.M. Each watch begins a new period consisting of eight bells. For example, noon is eight bells, twelve-thirty is one bell, and one o'clock is two bells.

Why is a fish used as a Christian symbol?

This sign is seen on altar cloths, on religious jewelry, and even on bumper stickers. It did not arise as testimony to the miracle of loaves and fishes, as you might think. The fact is that the first letters of the Greek words "Jesus Christ, Son of God, Savior" form the Greek word for fish. The idea that the acrostic came first is generally accepted, but it may be that the symbol came first, as it is found in very ancient catacombs and monuments.

Why does a groom carry his bride over the threshold?

Today this romantic act is thought to bring good luck, although it actually began with marriage by capture, when primitive man *had* to carry—or drag—his mate home. The ancient Romans observed this practice because of their belief in spirits. They thought two spirits, one good and one evil, waited inside the door. The evil spirit, always jealous of human happiness, hoped to trip the bride as she entered and ruin her happiness, since tripping was a very bad omen. The Romans also believed that a kind spirit followed at each person's right side and an evil one at the left. If a nervous bride stepped into the house on her left foot, the evil spirit would be able to enter. The only way the husband could be sure that wouldn't happen was to carry her over the threshold!

Why do we say "according to Hoyle"?

Edmond Hoyle (1672–1769) was an English writer on card games. It is believed that he earned his livelihood by playing card games in taverns, particularly whist. In 1742 he published *A Short Treatise on the Game of Whist* and later wrote a general book on games. Hoyle was considered the foremost authority on whist, and later, games in general. Thus, playing a game "according to Hoyle" means that one is playing according to its recognized rules.

Why is the bald eagle the national symbol?

The search for a national emblem led naturally to the eagle. As far back as 3000 B.C. it had been used as a symbol of power and courage. The Sumerians used it, as did the ancient Romans, the emperor Charlemagne, and Napoleon. The bald eagle, native only to the continent of North America, was chosen as an emblem of the new nation. It is not called bald because it has a featherless head, by the way. The term "bald" originally meant "white," as this eagle has a white-feathered head.

Why does a year have twelve months?

Before man figured out how to measure a solar year, time was marked by moons. It was the Egyptians who realized that twelve new moons equal four seasons, or one year. They also noticed that just about every twelve moons the brilliant star Sirius rose before the sun. The period of time between Sirius' risings was 365 days. This observation led to the establishment of a 365-day year divided into 12 months, each with 30 days, with five days left over at the end of the year. Variants of the twelve-month calendar occurred among other ancient peoples. The Roman calendar, from which ours is derived, went through many changes. It was Julius Caesar who ended the confusion by adopting a calendar based on a solar year of 365¼ days, with a leap year to take care of the extra quarter day.

Why did the Chinese bind women's feet?

Like a fair complexion, thin eyebrows, and a gentle voice, the Chinese considered the mincing walk of a woman whose feet were bound to be attractive. Small feet were also admired in themselves, so much so that it eventually became almost impossible to marry off a daughter with large (unbound) feet. Bound feet had another advantage on the marriage market: they kept the women at home.

Introduced as early as the tenth century A.D., foot binding was first practiced only by the upper classes. Later it became general, and was adopted even by peasant families. Only a pauper, determined to keep his daughter as a laborer, would consider not binding her feet—and thereby ruining her chances of ever marrying.

Why do we refer to a hidden advantage as an "ace in the hole"?

In poker, a "hole" card is one that is left facedown on the table and not exposed until the betting is over. An "ace in the hole" is thus a secret advantage or hidden strength.

Why is a weak spot referred to as an "Achilles' heel"?

Achilles, the Greek mythological hero, was noted for his strength, bravery, and beautiful physique. In *The Iliad,* his mother, Thetis, had a premonition that her son would die in battle. So she dipped him in the River Styx to make him invulnerable. Thetis held the infant by his heel while the rest of his body was immersed in the water. As fate would have it, a poison arrow shot by Apollo wounded Achilles in the heel, his only vulnerable spot, and caused his death.

Throughout the centuries people have been referring to a weak or vulnerable spot as an "Achilles' heel." In fact, in physiology the strong muscle connecting the calf of the leg with the heel is known as *tendo Achillis,* the tendon of Achilles.

Why is a financial backer called an "angel"?

The first "angel," some experts claim, was Luis de Santangel. He is said to be the man who actually financed Christopher Columbus' voyage to the New World. According to this version, Ferdinand and Isabella put Columbus off so many times that he finally took De Santangel's money and left. A shortened version of De Santangel—*angel*—is now used to describe those who back theatrical productions.

Why do we say "the apple of his eye"?

In ancient times the pupil of the eye was conceived of as a solid globe, and called the apple. Since injury to the pupil results in blindness, the pupil—or apple—came to represent anything that one cherishes most.

Why do we say "as the crow flies"?

The common belief is that a crow flies in a straight line from its starting point to its destination, while a person on the ground must go around buildings, over hills, etc., and cover a greater distance to get to the same place. Those who have observed crows, however, know that in fact they zigzag a good deal in their flight.

Why do we use the phrase "an ax to grind"?

The story behind this phrase is given in Benjamin Franklin's essay "Too Much for Your Whistle." A man came to Franklin professing an interest in how a grindstone works. Using the visitor's dull ax, Franklin demonstrated the grindstone. Finally the ax was sharp, but Franklin was worn out. The man, whose objective all along had been to have his ax sharpened, only laughed at Franklin. Nowadays anyone who, like Franklin's visitor, has "an ax to grind" is one who has a secret motive behind what he professes.

Why is thirteen called a "baker's dozen"?

Bread baking and selling were tightly regulated in England during the Middle Ages. It may be that this phrase grew out of some bakers' custom of giving an extra loaf with each dozen so that they would not be fined for underweight. The older name for thirteen was "Devil's dozen," a reference to the belief that witches gather in covens of thirteen to receive orders from the Devil.

Why do we say "barking up the wrong tree"?

This expression became popular in the nineteenth century, and in its literal sense referred to a coon hunt. Coons, being nocturnal animals, are hunted at night, and if chased will climb a tree. The hound is expected to bay at the foot of the tree until the hunter gets there. But it is possible for the dog to lose the coon by choosing the wrong tree in the dark. Thus, someone who "barks up the wrong tree" is going in the wrong direction or after the wrong thing.

Why is it called "barnstorming"?

The original "barnstormers" were actors who toured the country, performing anywhere they could find an audience. If there wasn't a theater in the vicinity, they might use a barn. As for the "storms," they were the loud, dramatic speeches and vigorous movements such actors favored. In the late nineteenth century the term also came to be applied to those who toured the country in whirlwind political campaigns.

Why do we say "red tape"?

The term "red tape" refers to official inaction or delay caused by bureaucratic shuffle (most notably government, institutions, and big business). It originated in England in the nineteenth century, when it was customary to tie official and legal documents with a tape of a pinkish-red color. Harassed by officials who delayed government decisions by giving undue attention to routine and hiding behind excuses for their rules and regulations, the common man ridiculed the process of tying and untying red tape that bound the dispatch and document cases in public offices.

Why do we give people "the cold shoulder"?

It's an act of unfriendliness to give somebody the cold shoulder, and that's exactly what it was in medieval France. Serving guests a hot roast was the cordial custom, but when a guest outstayed his welcome, or was obnoxious to the host, a cold shoulder of mutton or beef was served in lieu of the hot meal. Yes, even in those days it was an unfriendly gesture to give somebody the cold shoulder.

Why do we say "best foot forward"?

This phrase pays homage to an ancient belief that the right side is rational and free from dangerous emotions, while the left side is emotional because it is ruled by the heart. For this reason, stepping forward on the right foot was a sort of charm against failure or bad luck. The Roman form of this superstition was that each person was followed by two spirits, a good one on the right side and an evil one on the left. If a person stepped into a building with the right foot first, the kindly spirit came in with him rather than the evil one. So strongly did the Romans believe this that guards stood at the doors to important public buildings to make sure people stepped in "best foot forward." Beliefs of this sort survived longest among seafaring men, who always stepped onto a new ship with the right foot first to insure a safe maiden voyage.

Why is New York City called "The Big Apple"?

By 1971, according to the New York Convention and Visitors Bureau, New York City's image was at its lowest. It was called "Crime City" or "Fear City." "The Big Apple" is a deliberate attempt by the Bureau to create for New York City an image "with pleasant, positive connotations . . . a bright and shining image." But the Bureau did not invent the term. It originated in the early twentieth century among jazz musicians. They had a saying: "There are many apples on the tree, but to play in New York City is to play The Big Time . . .The Big Apple!"

Why do we say "to the bitter end"?

This common phrase has nothing to do with bitterness as we generally use it, but comes from the nautical word "bitt," which is a post on which cables and ropes—including the anchor cable— are wound. The end of the cable that is wrapped around the post is called "the bitter end." So the phrase has come to mean the very end, the absolute limit.

Why do we use the word "blackball"?

The original of this word was literal. In many private clubs black balls were used to vote against admitting a new member. If all the balls in the voting box were white, the member was in. But even one black ball meant he would be rejected. It is only natural that the term is now used to signify either a negative vote or exclusion from a social group.

Why do we use the term "blacklist"?

The practice of blacklisting began in the Middle Ages with "black books." At British universities the names of students guilty of misconduct were recorded in such books. Merchants used them to itemize people who were poor credit risks. The first "black lists" as such were lists of bankrupts. In modern times the black list was commonly circulated as a "don't hire" list. Employers used it against men who joined unions. The most famous blacklist was in Hollywood during the post-World War II period. Actors, writers, and many others who worked in the entertainment industry were added to these lists if they were suspected of Communist sympathies. During the McCarthy era it was revealed that black-listing had made it impossible for many talented people to find work in their fields.

Why do aristocrats have "blue blood"?

While no human being has blood any color other than various shades of red, the term "blue blood" comes from Spanish social history. During the fifteenth century, most Spanish aristocrats were blond, and due to their fair complexions their veins looked bluer than those of people of darker pigmentation, especially the Moorish and Jewish people. Thus, certain families of Castile claimed to have blue blood, a mark of superiority.

Why are they called "blue jeans"?

This popular item of clothing is known by several names. "Jeans" does not refer to a girl but to Genoa, a town where the cloth was once woven, "Denim" also refers to a place—Nîmes, France, where serge de Nîmes was manufactured. In Hindustan, *dungri* was a coarse woven fabric used to make sails. When sailors made work clothes from this fabric, they called them "dungarees." "Levis" were named after Levi Strauss, a clothing merchant in Gold Rush San Francisco. His most noteworthy additions to the garment were rivets at the corners of the pockets so that they wouldn't tear when miners filled them with ore.

Why are twelve inches called a "foot"?

Our units of measurement derive from very early standards, all relating to the human body. The Egyptians, for instance, used the *cubit* to build the pyramids. A cubit was the distance from the elbow to the end of the middle finger. The *inch* was the length of the index finger from tip to first joint, and it so happened that twelve of them equaled approximately a *foot*—which was just what it says, the length of a foot. The *yard* was the length of a man's arm. And the *mile* was originally a thousand paces, or double steps.

Why do we say "blow hot and cold"?

This expression, which means wavering between two alternatives, comes from a fable by Aesop. One winter day a satyr met a traveler who was blowing on his fingers. When the satyr asked him why, the man said it warmed his fingers. The satyr took the man home and served him a dish of hot pottage. The traveler blew on the pottage, explaining that it was too hot to eat and he was trying to cool it. At that, the satyr kicked him out of the cave, saying he wanted nothing to do with a man who could "blow hot and cold from the same mouth."

Why are state laws regulating the sale of stocks and bonds called "blue-sky laws"?

The Kansas legislature passed the first blue-sky law in 1911. During this period of speculation, the Kansas secretary of state required investment companies to file a full description of their business activities, and until authorized by the state bank commissioner, their securities could not be sold. One member of the committee declared that, if given the opportunity, the wildcat promoters would capitalize the blue skies. Another committee member then argued that the restrictions on investment firms should be "as far-reaching as the blue sky."

Why are London policemen called "bobbies"?

When Sir Robert Peel became Home Secretary, he created the Metropolitan Police Force. The people, who saw the force as a body created to suppress legitimate discontent, called it "Peel's bloody gang." Later the police were called "peelers" and "bobbies," and as time passed, the nicknames lost their derogatory impact. Today the people of Great Britain affectionately call their policemen bobbies.

Why is a heavy reader called a "bookworm"?

There actually *are* bookworms. Found in old, undusted libraries, they are the larvae of insects that feed on the paste in book bindings. Because they are always found around books—and sometimes seem to "devour" them—avid readers are called bookworms.

Why is the sale of illegal liquor called "bootlegging"?

The sale of illegal liquor originated in the Far West, when it was unlawfully sold on the reservations to the Indians. Often, flasks of firewater were carried in the violator's boots in order to conceal the merchandise from government officials. When prohibition laws were passed in various parts of the country, the term "bootlegging" was applied to the illegal sale of liquor.

Why do we call liquor "booze"?

Some people believe the word "booze" goes back to the Philadelphia distiller E. S. Booz, whose name appears on old whiskey bottles. But "booze" was already in use in the fourteenth century, when "to booze" meant "to drink heavily." Incidentally, while Americans use "booze" to mean hard liquor, the English use it to mean beer or ale.

Why do we speak of "boycotting"?

This word comes from the name of Captain Charles Boycott. When he attempted to collect high rents from the earl of Earne's poor tenants, the Irish farmers ignored—or boycotted—the captain.

Why do we use the term "the boys in the backroom"?

This phrase was first used by Lord Beaverbrook in 1941. In a speech he praised "the boys in the backroom." The expression is still used to refer to those who do nitty-gritty research in the sciences and technology and who are never in the public eye.

Why do we say "break the ice"?

In winter and in arctic regions it is necessary to break up ice for ships to get through. The phrase was already used figuratively by the late sixteenth century. Now it is a common metaphor meaning

to break down reserve between people, particularly new acquaintances.

Why do we say "bringing home the bacon"?

Some experts think this phrase refers to catching the greased pig at a county fair. The winner got to keep the pig, thus "bringing home the bacon." A second explanation is that the phrase is just a figure of speech, in which "bacon" stands for food in general, as "bread" does in "breadwinner." "Bringing home the bacon" has now broadened to mean general success in a venture, as well as simply bringing home the means of support.

Why do we believe a change in the moon brings a change in the weather?

This common belief is incorrect. The phases of the moon are the same everywhere, but weather in different parts of the world varies. Ancient people believed the actual shape of the moon changed with each phase. Perhaps someone observed a few coincidental changes of moon and weather, and decided there was a cause-and-effect relationship.

Why do we say "brand-new"?

This phrase has nothing to do with name brands, but goes back to the Middle Ages. Then a "brand" was a flame. When a metal product was taken right out of the flames, it was "fire-new" or "brand-new."

Why is a dollar called a "buck"?

American furriers classified skins as "bucks" and does." Bucks, being larger, were worth more. By 1850, the term "buck," meaning a dollar, had come into wide use.

Why is a golf course referred to as "links"?

The Art of Golfe by Sir W. J. Simpson, written in 1892, stated: "The grounds on which golf is played are called links, being the barren sandy soil from which the sea has retired in recent geological times. In their natural state, links are covered with long, rank, bent grass and gorse—These links are too barren for cultivation, but sheep, rabbits, geese and professionals pick up a precarious livelihood on them." Of course, today some of the best links are found in deserts and mountainous areas throughout the world.

Why do we say "bury the hatchet"?

This phrase is used to describe the settlement of a conflict and the beginning of friendly relations. There was a similar saying in England, dating from the fourteenth century: "hang up the hatchet." Some authorities believe this is the origin of the phrase. But there is also an American Indian ritual in which burying two axes in the ground signified a binding peace treaty. "This," Samuel Sewell wrote in 1680, was "more significant . . . than all the Articles of Peace."

Why is underwear called "BVDs"?

There have been a lot of theories as to what these letters stood for. Some said "Baby's Ventilated Diapers" and some said "Boy's Ventilated Drawers." But the simple truth is that these initials stood for the names of the men who organized the company— Bradley, Voorhies, and Day.

Why are secondary laws called "bylaws"?

"Bylaws" are secondary laws, or laws governing the internal affairs of an organization. The *by* in "bylaw" comes from an old Danish word, *bye* or *by,* meaning "town." The names of many

English villages, especially in Lincolnshire, which was a Danish settlement, end in *by*. "Bylaws," then, were the laws of the village, as distinguished from the laws of the kingdom. From this, the word gradually came to refer to any sort of minor regulation.

Why are ballboys called "caddies" in golf?

Mary, who became Queen of Scots in 1542, was an avid golfer. As a young girl she was sent to France to be educated. She referred to the ball chasers as "cadets"—the young pupils who carried her golf clubs. In France, "cadets" was pronounced "cad-day," and the term "caddie" was soon adopted. It is not known what these golf ballboys were called prior to Mary's visit to France.

Why is the childbirth operation called a "Caesarean"?

Many people think this operation was so named because Julius Caesar was delivered by this method. In fact, he was not. The Romans did not use this operation on living women. Roman law did permit such an operation after the mother's death. This was so the child might be delivered live, as occasionally happened, or so that mother and child could be buried separately, as their religion dictated. This law was part of a group of laws codified in 715 B.C. which, under the reign of the emperors, came to be known as the Caesarean Laws. The specific law that pertained to the childbirth operation was called the Caesarean Section.

Why do we use the expression "can't hold a candle to"?

It has been suggested that this expression has something to do with candling eggs—holding them to a light to examine them for freshness. Actually, the phrase goes back to the Renaissance. At that time, since there were no streetlights, a person walking home

after dark hired a "linkboy" to light the way with a candle or torch. Because the job was so menial, linkboys were considered inferior. So if you said John "couldn't hold a candle to" Bill, you were really saying that John was inferior even to a linkboy.

Why do we believe elephants fear mice?

The logic behind this superstition seems to be that an elephant fears that a mouse might run up the inside of his trunk. But elephants don't really mind mice. If mice are put in an elephant's immediate vicinity, he will sniff at them and then go back to whatever he was doing, to all appearances quite unconcerned.

Why is a stiff muscle called a "charley horse"?

Anyone can get a charley horse, although it is more common among athletes who use their muscles strenuously. In a charley horse, overstrained muscles suddenly contract into a stiff knot, and any exercise is very painful. The term derives from the custom of calling any old horse, especially one with stiff legs, a charley horse.

Why is a professional driver called a "chauffeur"?

Any student of French knows that *chauffer* means "to warm up." Why, then, do chauffeurs have that name? The first automobile drivers in France drove steam-propelled vehicles. Their job began with heating up the engine until enough steam was generated to propel the car. Thus they were called *chauffeurs,* or "warmers."

Why do we use the word "chauvinism" to describe blind loyalty?

Nicolas Chauvin was a soldier in Napoleon's army. After being wounded seventeen times he was retired on a meager pension. Nevertheless, he was fanatically devoted to Napoleon and praised him constantly. "Chauvinist" came to mean anyone who is blindly loyal to a group, especially to his country.

Why do we say "chew the rag"?

This slang expression means to talk at length, argue, or discuss. "Rag" here doesn't refer to a strip of cloth, but comes from the eighteenth-century verb "to rag," meaning "to scold." "Chew," in the sense of chewing words, is used by Shakespeare. Angelo in *Measure for Measure* chews a name—that is, repeats it over and over.

Why is the chicken dish called "chicken á la king"?

While there are dozens of stories that explain this name, the two most persuasive ones suggest that the dish was originally "Chicken á la Keene." The London hotel, Claridge's, claims that its chef invented it in 1881 to honor sportsman J. R. Keene after his horse won the Grand Prix. But the New York restaurant Delmonico's has also been cited as the originator; there the dish was supposed to have been suggested by Keene's son, Foxhall Keene. As numerous restaurants adopted the dish, many must have wanted to suggest that it was fit for royalty—hence, "Chicken á la King."

Why is the chinese dish called "chop suey"?

In New York, on August 29, 1896, the Chinese statesman Li Hung-Chang had his chef create *chop suey*, which at that time was unknown in China. It was an attempt to create a dish that would appeal to both American and Oriental tastes. In Chinese, *chop suey* means miscellaneous bits of food, like a hash.

Why is a beer can opener called a "church key"?

Many people suppose the term "church key," describing the kind of opener that punches a triangle in a can of beer, reflects a mock reverence for the brew. Actually, the present church key replaced an older kind of bottle opener of the same name. That device looked like the top end of one of the large, ornate keys used to open church doors. When cans became common, today's church key gained in popularity, and the name was transferred to it.

Why do we say "cock-and-bull story"?

This refers to any story that is unbelievable. One such tale was told in 1660 by Samuel Fisher, about a cock and a bull being transformed into a single animal. This story seemed so incredible that people may have used "cock-and-bull story" to refer to one so unbelieveable that it must have been invented. In any case, the phrase was immortalized by Laurence Sterne in *Tristram Shandy*. The last words of this classic novel are: "What is all this story about?—A Cock And a Bull, said Yorick—and one of the best of its kind I ever heard."

Why do we use the term "come to a head"?

When something comes to a head, we know something is about to happen. This expression came about because of the medieval notion that cabbage resembled a human head. In fifteenth-century England cabbage was a major item in the diet of the poor. Cabbage, in its early stages, has large loose leaves and looks like a green flower; only when it ripens do the inside leaves wrap tightly about each other, so that it begins to look like a head.

For the poor and hungry, waiting for this slow-maturing plant to come to market must have been difficult. We can imagine people going to a farmer to buy cabbage, only to be told, "We have to wait till it comes to a head."

Why do we call waiting "cooling one's heels"?

The original of this expression seems to be "to cool one's hoofs." It goes back to the time when the horse was the principal means of transportation. During a long journey the horse's hoofs would actually become heated and painful, and the driver or horseman would have to give the animal a chance to cool its hoofs. Since this meant waiting, the expression came to have that meaning. Applied to humans, it became "cool one's heels," and to this day means a forced waiting period.

Why do we call policemen "cops"?

Two theories account for this term. One points to the old English verb "to cop," meaning catch. If this is the derivation, a policeman was originally a "copper," or "cop" for short, in the sense that he cops or captures criminals. A more interesting theory refers to the time when Sir Robert Peel organized the first modern police force. He dressed the men in blue uniforms with conspicuous copper buttons. These buttons, some say, led to the nickname "coppers," later shortened to "cops."

Why do we refer to a "Cook's tour"?

A "Cook's tour" today may refer to any kind of pleasure trip. The original, however, was a tour organized by Cook's, the oldest and largest travel agency in the world. Cook's was started in 1841 by Thomas Cook, an ardent teetotaler. When the Midlands County

Railway opened an extension between Leighborough and Leicester, he persuaded the company to greatly reduce the fare if he would guarantee five hundred passengers. Both sides kept the bargain, and 570 teetotalers made a 48-mile round trip for 14 cents each— the start of a travel empire.

Why is the game called "craps"?

Two theories explain how the game of craps got its name. One is that a Creole gambler, nicknamed Johnny Crapaud, introduced the game to New Orleans. There it became known as "Crapaud's game," later shortened to "craps." A second theory refers to an old dice game called "hazard." "Crabs," or "craps," in this game was the lowest possible throw. "Crap out" is still used the same way in the modern game, so this explanation seems more likely.

Why is an unexpected winner called a "dark horse"?

Benjamin Disraeli, the distinguished English prime minister, was also a well-known writer. Among his works was a three-volume novel, *The Young Duke: A Moral Tale Though Gay*. In volume two the book's main character attends a horse race. He is amazed to see "a dark horse" he hadn't noticed before sweep past the judge's box to win first place. During the time this novel was popular, the "dark horse" the Duke observed came to stand for any winner whose victory no one predicts. And it still has the same meaning.

Why do we say "dead as a doornail"?

The first person to say "dead as a . . ." must have searched for some common, totally lifeless object to complete the metaphor.

During the Middle Ages doors were ornamented with nails, so they were easily visible items and an obvious comparison. The phrase occurs as early as 1363 in *Piers Plowman,* and is also found in Shakespeare. The alliteration—repetition of the *d* sound—is probably as responsible as anything for keeping this old phrase alive.

Why is a soldier called a "dogface"?

Most dictionaries say this slang term sprang up in World War II. It is true that at that time Bill Mauldin's cartoon characters introduced the word to the general public. It had, however, been around for a long time. One military source claims it goes back to the days of the Indian Wars. The Indians coined the word because they thought the Sheridan forage cap the soldiers wore gave them doglike profiles.

Why do we refer to discarding items as "deep sixing"?

To "deep six" is a nautical term meaning to bury at sea in six or more fathoms of water. It was during the Watergate scandal that the term was used to mean getting rid of incriminating material in any way possible.

Why is a race called a "derby"?

The word "derby" is used to refer to various horse races, such as the Kentucky Derby, and even to other kinds of races, such as the Soapbox Derby. But the original Derby—pronounced *Darby*—is the race at Epsom Downs in Surrey, England. This race was started by the twelfth Earl of Derby, an enthusiastic sportsman who lived in Epsom. For variety, the Earl proposed a race for three-year-old fillies at Epsom Downs. His suggestion was cheered, as was his idea the next year of opening the race to colts as well. In his honor, the fashionable race was named after him—the Derby.

Why is a short-barreled pistol called a "derringer"?

The derringer is perhaps best known as the gun that John Wilkes Booth used to shoot Lincoln. The original derringer was a little box-lock pistol made by Henry Deringer, a gunsmith, in the 1840s. So great was the demand for the gun that a California agent hired former apprentices of Deringer to make imitations of it. These were signed *J. Deringer,* after a tailor who was paid for the use of his name. On the foreign imitations which soon appeared, "Derringer" was spelled with two *r*'s. The latter spelling is now standard, referring to any short-barreled pistol.

Why do we say "The die is cast"?

"Die" in this expression is the singular of *dice,* so that the phrase refers to casting dice, as in shooting craps. While many people think "the die is cast" means that a pattern, or die, has been cast in metal to make a mold, the phrase is much older than the use of dies in metalworking. In fact, when Caesar crossed the Rubicon he is supposed to have said, *"Jacta alea est"* ("The dice have been thrown")—in other words, there is no changing things now.

Why do we call an ornamental mat a "doily"?

During the early eighteenth century, a Londoner named Doily amassed a fortune from selling linens and crocheted goods. His fast rise to riches became so famous that the "doily" was named after him.

Why do we call being cheated being "double crossed"?

When a person is "crossed up," he is somehow cheated or let down. A double cross, then, implies that a cheater is betrayed. And this was the meaning of an early form of the phrase, "to put on the double-double." A term familiar in racing circles, it meant cheating someone who believes he has fixed a race. Nowadays to "double cross" means to betray someone by failing to go through with a course of action previously agreed upon.

Why are a pair of aces with a pair of eights called "a dead man's hand" in poker?

It is believed that when James Butler Hickok ("Wild Bill") was shot by Jack McCall during a poker game in Deadwood, South Dakota, on August 2, 1876, he held such a hand. Although it was an unfortunate event for law-enforcement officer Hickok, many poker players believe that a dead man's hand is very lucky and is seldom beaten.

Why do we call the South "Dixie"?

"Dixie" may be derived simply from the Mason-*Dixon* line. But a more ingenious explanation traces it to *"dix"*—the French word for "ten." "Dix" used to be displayed in large letters on a bilingual ten-dollar bill issued by a bank in New Orleans. The bills gained the nickname "dixies." Since having ten dollars in the South's most colorful city was a pleasant sensation, some Southerners saw

"Dixie" as a positive name for the South. When Daniel Emmet's song "Dixie" became popular in 1859, the term rapidly spread throughout the country.

Why do we call a skeptic a "doubting Thomas"?

A "doubting Thomas" is a person who has to be shown in order to believe. St. Thomas, the apostle, was the first doubting Thomas. According to the Bible (John 20), Thomas would not believe that Christ had risen from the dead until he had actually seen and touched the wounds of the Crucifixion.

Why do we hold a baseball bat with the trademark facing away from the pitcher?

Bat manufacturers place the trademark so that it runs *with* the grain of the wood. If this spot is hit by a fast ball, it is more likely to split than if the same ball were to hit the other side of the bat.

Why do we call it a "drawing room"?

Originally, a drawing room was not a place to sketch, but rather a place to *with*draw to. "Withdrawing room" was later contracted to "drawing room."

Why do we say "drink a toast"?

In Elizabethan England it was customary to put a bit of toast in a glass of wine to improve its flavor. One day a noted beauty was in the public bath, and an admirer drank her health with a glass of the water she stood in. Another admirer said he did not like the liquor but wanted the toast. Thereafter, ladies were for a time called *"toasts,"* and at dinners it was customary to drink their health. This custom came to be known as "toasting."

Why do we say "dyed in the wool"?

This old expression refers to textiles. Color will last better if wool is dyed in its raw state, before it is made into yarn. A person whose habits are "dyed in the wool" is inflexible, and cannot be easily changed any more than the color in such wool.

Why do we say "eating crow"?

To "eat crow" is to be forced into a humiliating situation. The phrase was inspired by an incident that took place during the War of 1812 along the Niagara River. It was common for soldiers of both sides to go hunting during an armistice. One New Englander, crossing the river, shot a crow when he could not find larger game. An unarmed British officer heard the shot and decided the intruder must be punished. Since he himself had no weapon, the officer complimented the soldier on his shooting and his gun, then asked to see the weapon. When the naive soldier handed it over, the officer aimed it at him and ordered him to eat a bite of the crow. The soldier, unable to talk him out of it, had to comply. The officer then warned him to stay on his own side of the river, and handed back his gun. But the soldier stopped him from returning to camp by pointing the gun at him and ordering him to eat the rest of the crow.

The next day the British officer went to the American commander and told his side of the story, demanding that the soldier who violated the armistice be punished. The captain had the soldier brought in and asked him whether he had ever before seen the British officer. It was reported that the soldier answered, "Why, yes, Captain, I dined with him yesterday."

Why do we say a prosperous person is "eating high off the hog"?

When someone is living well—particularly after working his way up from poverty—we say he is "eating high off the hog." This metaphor actually began as literal description, for the best and most expensive cuts of pork, such as the loin, are located high up on the hog.

Why do we say "eat humble pie"?

Although this phrase means to apologize for something or to be humiliated, it doesn't come from "humble" as we use the word today. The "humbles," or "numbles," are edible organs of an animal. It was once customary to make a meat pie of these organs for the common huntsmen and servants. So if you ate humble pie, you were a person without rank.

Why do we say "face the music"?

This picturesque phrase refers to accepting the consequences of one's behavior, particularly unpleasant consequences. It may have originated in the military, referring to foot soldiers standing in formation facing the band, or to cavalrymen, whose horses must be kept under control facing the band. Another military explanation is that a cavalryman who was given a dishonorable discharge was literally drummed out of camp, in which case he was facing the rear end of his horse as well as the drum music. The most popular explanation of "face the music," however, is that it originated in the theater. There the actor, no matter how nervous, must come onstage and face the orchestra directly below the footlights.

Why do we say "R.S.V.P."?

These initials are an abbreviation of the French phrase, *"Répondez s'il vous plait,"* which means, "Please reply."

Why do we say "a flash in the pan"?

The pan in question was a small depression in the old flintlock musket, whose hammer struck a flint, producing sparks. These sparks hopefully ignited powder in the pan, which burned and exploded the charge. But it was an uncertain process. Sometimes the powder in the pan just flashed and failed to ignite the charge. Anything showy that promises great success but fails is still called "a *flash in the pan*."

Why do we say "a feather in his cap"?

The practice of putting a feather in the cap as a symbol of achievement goes back to the Middle Ages. In 1346 Edward, "the Black Prince," distinguished himself in the Battle of Crécy, where the English seemed hopelessly outnumbered. After the English victory Edward was awarded the crest of John, King of Bohemia. This crest of three ostrich feathers thereafter became the badge of every Prince of Wales. It also became customary for any knight who had distinguished himself—especially on the battlefield—to wear a feather in his helmet. By the fifteenth century, all members of the English nobility wore feathers on their headgear as a symbol of their distinction.

Why do we refer to high society as "the four hundred"?

Ward McAllister, a leader of New York society, started this fashion. In 1889 he said only four hundred people in the city could gracefully enter a ballroom. He also said, more sweepingly, that there were only about four hundred persons in New York's best social circles. A few years later he boasted that he had helped cut down the guest list for the Astor ball to four hundred. The press and the public picked up the number, and "four hundred" in the sense of "top society" became part of the language.

Why do we say "a good break"?

This phrase, as well as "a bad break" and "an even break," was born in the poolroom. To start a game, the players rack the balls up into a triangle. The first player "breaks," or shoots the cue ball into this triangle. If he sinks some balls, that's "a good break."

Why do we say "get down to brass tacks"?

Some sources say the "brass tacks" in this phrase were driven into the counters of old-fashioned general stores exactly a yard apart. When a woman bought yard goods, rather than guessing at the amount of fabric, she could use the tacks to measure precisely. Another theory refers to nineteenth-century upholstered furniture. It seems the upholstering process began with brass tacks. If something went wrong with the furniture, the way to approach it was to check the foundation—or "get down to brass tacks."

Why do we speak of "the brush-off"?

If you are passed up by somebody, snubbed, or pointedly ignored, you've been "brushed off." This expression has been traced back to the Pullman porter. If he had reason to think a person was a poor tipper, he would just give him a few passes with his lint brush and move on to a better prospect.

Why do we say a high-spirited person is "feeling his oats"?

This American expression has been around since at least 1831, when it can be found recorded in the Boston *Transcript*. It was first said, naturally, of horses, who may become spirited after a nourishing meal of oats. Now it is used to describe anyone who acts in an energetic fashion.

Why do we say "go haywire"?

"To go haywire" is to function erratically or improperly, to break down. The "haywire" in question is baling wire, used to tie up bales of hay. There are two ways this wire relates to the phrase as we use it. First, the easiest way to remove haywire so the hay can be used is by striking it with a hatchet. When you do, the wire springs out and whirls about erratically. As for the breaking down also referred to by this expression, haywire is used on farms for temporary repairs of every sort. A property where everything is broken and mended this way might be said to have "gone haywire."

Why do we say "gone to pot"?

Something (or someone) that is no longer what it used to be has gone to pot. The "pot" in this phrase may be a stewing pot. Meat that has been chopped up and used for stew is not what it once was—it has literally gone to the pot. Another source suggests the "pot" is a trash can, specifically one for waste metal. A third possibility is that "pot" refers to the urn used to hold the ashes of the dead. This latter explanation is most likely, since early writers often used "gone to pot" to mean that someone had died.

Why is New York called "Gotham"?

The original Gotham is a village in Nottinghamshire, England. The legend is that in order to prevent King John from establishing a residence nearby—which they feared would raise their taxes—all of the Gothamites feigned madness. The King's messengers found some of them trying to confine a cuckoo within a bush by joining hands around it, others attaching a cart to a barn to shade the shingles, still others trying to drown eels, etc. The King's advance agents told him upon their return that there was no use settling in a village of fools. It was Washington Irving who first called

New York city Gotham, as a satire upon its citizens. The name has stuck, but as a synonym rather than a pejorative term.

Why do we call Greenland "green"?

Greenland, the largest island in the world, is mostly covered by ice and snow, and should therefore have appropriately been named "Whiteland." It is believed that in A.D. 985 Eric the Red named it Greenland to induce colonists from Iceland to inhabit the new island. Others believe that Eric the Red was not actually conning his followers, but was unaware of its ice-covered interior plateau, since he may have only visited Greenland's ice-free western coast in midsummer.

Why are unskilled Oriental laborers called "coolies"?

Kuli was the name of an Indian caste whose members hired out as unskilled labor, carrying burdens, bricks, and earth. Europeans in India took to calling all unskilled laborers "kulis." Some authorities think the term "coolie" derives from this usage. Others think it is a combination of two Chinese words: koo (painful) and lee (strength). In any case, in the early nineteenth century the term came to be applied specifically to unskilled workers from the Orient.

Why are Americans called "gringos"?

Most experts agree that gringo—a contemptuous Mexican word for foreigners, especially Americans and Englishmen—comes from the Spanish griego, or Greek. This was used in the sense of gibberish, as we say, "It's all Greek to me." Another school of thought, however, traces the word to Major Samuel Ringgold, who fought in the Mexican War under General Zachary Taylor. His bravery was well known, and he and his flying artillery corps were widely feared by Mexican marauders. When Ringgold is pronounced with a Spanish accent, it sounds much like *gringo*.

Why is a man called a "guy"?

"Guy" as a slang term for a man was not always as neutral as it is now. The word goes back to the famous Gunpowder Plot against the English Parliament in 1605. The conspirators, in retaliation against the oppression of Roman Catholics in Britain, placed 36 barrels of gunpowder in the basements of the Parliament buildings. On November 5, the day the King opened Parliament, they planned to set them off. But when Guy Fawkes went into the cellar to light the fuses, he was captured. The plot had become too widely known, and the conspiracy was revealed. November 5 became an English holiday, Guy Fawkes Day, celebrating the preservation of the government. Effigies of Fawkes were paraded through the streets and burned in huge bonfires. Celebrants customarily dressed in costumes similar to American Halloween costumes. A "guy" first meant any effigy, such as that of Guy Fawkes. Later it came to mean any odd-looking person. Over time, the term was used for "good guys" as well as "bad guys," until it became American slang for any man—or (in some unisex circles) woman.

Why do we say "hair of the dog"?

Since the sixteenth century this phrase has been used to describe a morning drink to relieve a bad hangover. At that time it was believed that a person bit by a rabid dog had a greater chance to recover if a hair of that dog was bound upon the wound.

Why is a stamp of genuineness called a "hallmark"?

"Hallmark" today is often used to mean evidence of the character of something, as in Theodor Reik's statement: "The sense of guilt is the hallmark of civilized humanity." Like many figurative terms, this one has literal origins. Centuries ago the Goldsmiths Hall in London appraised gold and silver items for genuineness and purity, and items that met its standards were stamped with the "hallmark."

Why is an actor who overacts called a "ham"?

A "ham" is an actor who is not just bad, but who also tries to draw attention to himself by overacting. The word may originate from the idea that such acting is amateurish, and Cockney English puts an *h* in front of "amateur," making it "hamateur." Another explanation is that actors once used fat to take off their makeup. But the most convincing theory connects the word to *Hamlet*. It was an old theatrical cliché that actors who were down on their luck bragged of having once done *Hamlet*. Moreover, Hamlet makes a speech to the players he assembles, warning them not to "strutt and bellow"—the very characteristics of the ham actor.

Why do people credit Horace Greeley with saying "Go west, young man"?

Greeley did repeat and publicize this admonition in his New York newspaper, the *Tribune*. But the originator was John Babsone Lane Soule, who first printed the advice in the Terre Haute *Express*. Because of Greeley's fame as a publisher and a candidate for the presidency of the United States, he is almost always given credit for the saying. The full sentence, by the way, was: "Go west, young man, and grow up with the country."

Why do we say "a chip on his shoulder"?

A man with "a chip on his shoulder" seems to be daring someone to fight with him. This expression comes from an old maxim: "Hew not too high lest chips fall in thine eye." In other words, don't chop too high on the tree. This became a way of applauding fearlessness; a brave man didn't worry about falling chips, or consequences. In America, the chip was seen as a literal chip placed on one's shoulder to warn an enemy against "hewing too high."

Why do we say "gets my goat"?

There are two interesting explanations for this peculiar phrase. One is that "goat" refers to a *"goatee,"* the pointed beard that resembles a goat's beard. Thus, if you *"get someone's goat"* you pull his beard, an insulting gesture. Another explanation comes from horse breeders, who point out that throughbred horses easily become attached to goats. A high-strung horse may calm down if a goat is kept in his stall. Such a horse may become nervous, however, if you take his goat away, or "get his goat."

Why do we say "hello"?

Over the centuries a number of similar words have been used to get the attention of a person some distance away. The first of these seems to be "hail," the sailor's call. This became "hallow" (with the accent on the second syllable), and then variously "hallo," "hilloo," and "hullo. "Hello" grew up in the United States as a way of answering the telephone. The salutation used at the first experimental switchboard, in 1878, was "Ahoy! Ahoy! "—which was originally the war cry of the Vikings. Following that, "Are you there?" was standard form for a short while. Thomas Edison's biographers tell us he was the first person to answer the telephone with "Hello," which immediately came into popular use.

Why do we speak of being left "holding the bag"?

In the sixteenth century the expression "to give the bag" was used to refer to a servant who left without notice, taking with him his master's cash and leaving behind only the empty purse or bag. Transformed in time into "holding the bag," it no longer means an empty bag. One left "holding the bag" today has all the responsibility or blame for something thrust on him alone.

Why is a wedding trip called a "honeymoon"?

Among the Teutons, a newly married couple drank mead (wine made with honey) for a period of about one month after the ceremony. That period of a month—or moon—put the *moon* in "honeymoon."

Why do we say "a horse of a different color"?

This expression, meaning another matter altogether, may have grown out of an English archaeological phenomenon, the White Horse of Berkshire, which is an outline of a horse 374 feet long, formed by trenches in a chalk hillside. It is customary for neighborhood citizens to clean the weeds from the trenches every so often, thus making it "a horse of a different color."

Why do we refer to a sure success as being "in the bag"?

Before 1920, when groceries were packaged in wrapping paper, the expression that meant certain success was "all wrapped up." When bags came into use, "in the bag" became a popular way of saying the same thing.

Why do we say "in the limelight"?

This phrase was originally theatrical slang. In 1825, a British Army officer, Thomas Drummond, served as assistant to the chief of the British trigonometrical survey. Drummond discovered the brilliant luminosity of incandescent lime while attending a series of lectures on chemistry and physics at the Royal Institution of London. While surveying northern Ireland, he used his "Drummond light," and later he adapted it for lighthouses. Soon afterward (since electricity had not yet been discovered) the theatre began to use Drummond footlights and floodlights. The part of the stage where the most important action occurred was referred to as the "limelight," and the leading actor was said to be "in the limelight." Today this expression applies to anybody, on- or offstage, who becomes the center of attention.

Why do we use the term "ivory tower"?

This term describes a place removed from the common world where intellectuals retire to think and study. The implication is that the occupant of an ivory tower is preoccupied with the theoretical and abstract at the expense of the practical. The original phrase was *un tour d'ivoire,* first used by Sainte-Beuve, the nineteenth-century French literary critic.

Why is it called the "Ivy League"?

It is commonly thought that this phrase is a reference to the ivy-covered walls some people associate with the old northeastern colleges. But the term actually goes back to the "Four League" of the mid-nineteenth century, an interscholastic league formed by Harvard, Yale, Princeton, and Columbia. The name of the league was always written in proper academic fashion in Roman numerals —IV League—and commonly pronounced as the Ivy League. The term came into general use in the 1930s after sportswriter Caswell Adams used it to refer to Princeton and Columbia. It wasn't until after World War II, however, that the northeastern schools formed what we now know as the Ivy League.

Why is a hare called a "jackrabbit"?

"Jackrabbit" comes from "jackass rabbit." This does not refer to the way the animal acts, but to its long ears, which are similar to those of the jackass. In the early West it was sometimes called the mule rabbit and sometimes—in a tribute to size—the Texas hare. But "jackass rabbit" caught on, and was eventually shortened to "jackrabbit."

Why are mid-block crossings called "jaywalking"?

Early in the twentieth century "jay" meant "countrified" or "newcomer." A rustic stranger to the city around that time might be easily confused by automobiles and traffic lights. Not understanding the signals, or ignoring them, he might very well cross the street illegally, or "jaywalk."

Why are small towns called "jerkwater"?

In the early days of railroads trains stopped at wayside streams for water. The practice was called "jerking water" because the water was carried in leather buckets, or "jerked," to the train. The original "jerkwater" town had nothing to recommend it except that trains could refill their water supply there. So "jerkwater" has come to be applied to any small or insignificant place.

Why do we say "The jig is up"?

The "jig" was a lively dance of very early origin. In seventeenth-century England the word "jig" also came to mean a trick or practical joke. So "the jig is up" means that the game is over, the trick is exposed.

Why do we say "keep the ball rolling"?

To "keep the ball rolling" is to keep a lively conversation going so that interest does not flag. The saying comes from the British game of bandy, which we call hockey. The game is played with a small ball rather than a disc-shaped puck. If that ball were not kept rolling, it would be a slow game and the spectators would lose interest.

Why do we say "keeping up with the Joneses"?

"Keeping up with the Joneses" was actually the name of a comic strip. The author, A. R. Momand, at first intended to call the strip "Keeping Up with the Smiths," but decided that "Joneses" sounded better. The strip was introduced in 1913 and ran until 1931.

Why are marines referred to as "leathernecks"?

At least two explanations are given for this term. The first—and least flattering—is a Navy tradition. Sailors believed that early marines did not strip to the waist to wash, as sailors did, but only rolled up their sleeves and washed their hands and face. Thus, "leatherneck" described a dirty, long-unwashed neck. A more likely explanation is that the name was suggested by marine uniforms of the nineteenth century. The regulation coat had a high, close-fitting collar lined with leather to keep it stiff. Because these collars were very uncomfortable when wet with perspiration, they were abandoned in the last quarter of the century. The term "leatherneck," however, persists.

Why is an unknown party called "John Doe"?

In legal actions we refer to an unknown person as "John Doe" or "Jane Doe." This use of "John Doe" began in England as early as the fourteenth century. The name sounds like a common one, as it was undoubtedly meant to, but is in fact very uncommon. There were only four Does in the 1981 Manhattan phone book, none of them with the first name of John. Compare that to some seventy John Smiths. The uncommonness of the name helps avoid confusion.

Why do we say "kick the bucket"?

One theory of the origin of "kick the bucket" refers to the process of slaughtering a pig. In England, hundreds of years ago, the newly killed pig was hung from a frame called a "bucket." If he still had some life in him he would kick around and, in his dying, "kick the bucket." The second explanation is that a bucket is an object a suicide might very well stand on as he fixes the rope around his neck. Then, in order to hang himself, he would have only to "kick the bucket" out from under him.

Why do we use the expression "knock off work"?

One of the most boring jobs of all time must have been that of the man who kept the oarsmen on a slave galley rowing in unison. He did so by tapping rhythmically on a block of wood. When the time came to change shifts, he gave a special pattern of knocks which signalled to the oarsmen that it was time to "knock off work."

Why do we say "know the ropes"?

A person who "knows the ropes" is familiar with all the details of
a job. If the phrase originated on the racetrack, as one authority
thinks, then "ropes" refers to the reins. Someone who knows how
to manipulate the reins, thereby handling the horse well, would
"know the ropes." Another theory is that the ropes in question are
on a sailing ship. As anyone who has ever tried to work those ropes
knows, they are not learned overnight. It's a good sailor who
"knows the ropes."

Why do we say "knuckle down"?

There are two theories of the origin of this phrase, both sound.
The first refers to the fact that "knuckle" at one time meant any
bone joint, including those on the spine. So "knuckling down"
meant putting your back into the job. Alternatively, "knuckle
down" may have come from the game of marbles. A rule of that
game is that a player must have his knuckles down—touching the
ground. When a match becomes hotly competitive a boy is likely to
press them even more firmly into the dirt to ensure a firm and
steady grip.

Why are sweet-sour beets called "Harvard beets"?

At one time Harvard was famous for its winning football teams.
When an unknown chef came up with the idea of beets in a
vinegar and sugar sauce, he thought the color very close to the
famous Harvard crimson, and named them "Harvard beets."

Why do we say "knuckle under"?

When you "knuckle under," you give in under pressure. The phrase
does not refer to the knuckles of the hands, but goes back to a

time when the larger joints—knee and elbow—were called "knuckles." Defeated in battle, a man would put his leg knuckles on the ground—that is, kneel before his conqueror.

Why do we say "lay an egg"?

This expression was first used by British cricket players. A score of zero was called a "duck's egg" because of the resemblance in shape. In America the idea was picked up in baseball, where a zero score became known as a "goose egg." The word "goose" was eventually dropped from the expression, and its use expanded so that "lay an egg" now means total failure in any field.

Why do we say "like a Dutch uncle"?

No one is sure whether this phrase, which is American in origin, referred to the Pennsylvania Dutch or the Dutch colonists in New York State. In both regions people were known to be severe disciplinarians. It could be assumed that, unlike most uncles, a Dutch uncle would be very stern with a child. The term "Dutch uncle" today has a different but similar meaning—somebody who takes a personal interest and watches over another person.

Why do we refer to "the lion's share"?

The person who gets the largest portion of anything is said to have "the lion's share." The expression derives from a fable by Aesop in which a lion, a fox, and an ass went hunting and killed a stag. The ass then divided it into three equal portions. But the lion took this as an insult to his dignity, and in a state of fury killed the ass. He then directed the fox to divide the stag. Craftier than the ass, the fox merely nibbled off a small piece for himself and left all the rest as "the lion's share."

Why do we say "lock, stock, and barrel"?

This phrase dates back to the American Revolution. The three parts of a gun are the lock, or firing mechanism, the stock, and the barrel. So if you have "lock, stock, and barrel," you have the entire gun, or the whole thing.

Why do we say "mad as a hatter"?

Although Lewis Carroll's Mad Hatter is famous, he derived the idea from a common folk saying. Everyone knew insanity was an occupational hazard of being a hatter, but no one knew why. It was Dr. Alice Hamilton, of Howard Medical School, who discovered that the nitrate of mercury that hatters used to treat felt was the culprit. People who worked in factories that used felt inhaled the vapors from this chemical, and sometimes the toxins affected the brain.

Why do we say "pull the wool over his eyes"?

At one time all gentlemen wore powdered wigs. "Wool" was then used as a slang term for hair. When the wool was pulled over a man's eyes, it meant that some jokester had pulled down his wig so he couldn't see. The present meaning of the expression is to deceive a person.

Why do we say "Mind your p's and q's"?

This expression means to be careful in what you're doing. The origin is much debated. One standard explanation is that it was said to printers' apprentices with respect to sorting type, since the only difference between the two letters is the direction of the tail.

Another possibility is that the expression goes back to the court of Louis XIV, where courtiers wore elaborate wigs or "queues." It is necessary to bow deeply as a sign of respect, while taking a step forward. In such a bow, the wig could fall off. Thus, one might be told to mind his p's (*pieds,* or feet) and q's (wig). A third explanation is that old English bars kept accounts with p for pint and q for quart. When the customer paid up, he might be overcharged if he was too tipsy to mind his "p's and q's."

Why is "Mrs." not an abbreviation?

"Mrs." is not an abbreviation, since it does not stand for anything, the way "Mr." does for "Mister." Originally it stood for "mistress," which at that time meant the woman who managed the house. But the meaning of "mistress" has changed so that it is no longer the equivalent of "wife."

Why do we say "the naked truth"?

This phrase appears in the writings of the Roman author Horace as *nuda veritas.* It comes from an old fable in which Falsehood stole the clothes Truth had left on the bank while swimming. Truth, unwilling to wear Falsehood's garments, chose to go naked.

Why do we say "namby-pamby"?

This word comes to us from the literary world of eighteenth-century England, when there was an ongoing feud between the admirers of Addison and those of Pope. When Ambrose Philips, a poet admired by Addison, wrote a highly sentimental poem, Pope scorned it. So did one Henry Carey, a musician and poet of the time. Carey wrote a parody of Philip's poem and titled it "Namby-Pamby." *Namby* was the nickname for Ambrose, and *Pamby* a reduplication suggested by his second initial. In this fashion the term, describing something sickeningly sentimental, came into the language.

Why do we say "a pig in a poke"?

To buy "a pig in a poke" is to buy an item sight unseen. This expression comes from England, where at one time the term "pig" was used only to refer to swine less than four months old. Such small pigs could be taken to market in a sack—called a "poke." It was common to try to sell the piglet without opening the bag; the excuse was that it would be very hard to catch if it escaped. But apparently some unprincipled people carried in the bag not a pig, but a worthless cat. A knowledgeable shopper would insist on actually seeing the pig—and sometimes that meant "letting the cat out of the bag!"

Why do we say "Never look a gift horse in the mouth"?

This expression refers, of course, to questioning the value of a gift. The number and condition of a horse's teeth tell its real age. So a person who looks in a gift horse's mouth is suggesting that the horse is older and less valuable than it looks. The first known use of this phrase was by St. Jerome in A.D. 400 in answer to his critics. Jerome, who never accepted payment for his writings, said: "Never inspect the teeth of a gift horse."

Why do we say "a Chinaman's chance"?

During the Gold Rush, over forty thousand Chinese came to work in California mining camps. Because they accepted very low wages and could not speak the language, they were not highly regarded. They had virtually no rights in miners' court, not even the right to plead self-defense. So "a Chinaman's chance" of surviving any charge was very small.

Why do we say "wet behind the ears"?

This homely expression means that someone is as naive as a newborn child. It comes from the farmyard, where anyone may observe that the depressions behind an animal's ears are the last places to dry after birth.

Why do we say "not worth a tinker's dam"?

In older writings, the last word of this phrase is sometimes "dam" and sometimes "damn," leading to two interpretations. One authority says that a tinker's dam was a pellet of bread used to plug a leak while a tinker poured in solder to repair it. This dam, which wasn't worth much in the first place, was totally worthless once it had been used, and had to be thrown away. A more common interpretation refers to the generally accepted belief that tinkers swore often while they were working. Thus, while another person's "damn!" might be taken seriously, a tinker's "damn!" would be disregarded.

Why do we say "the nth degree"?

This phrase refers to a quality of something, or someone, in an extreme or infinite degree—as in, "He was boring to the nth degree." The n in this phrase is a mathematical symbol. In an infinitely increasing series of numbers or values, n is the final item.

Why do we call movie awards "Oscars"?

For several years the trophies handed out annually by the Academy of Motion Picture Arts and Sciences were nameless. It was Margaret Herrick, librarian for the Academy, who supplied the name. When first shown a trophy she said, "It reminds me of my uncle Oscar." The name stuck.

Why do we abbreviate "ounce" as "oz."?

Scribes in the Middle Ages used a character similar to z at the end of all abbreviated words. When printing began, there was no special type for this symbol, so the printers used the nearest thing— the letter z. We get "oz." from the first letter of "ounce" plus this abbreviation sign.

Why do we say "pass the buck"?

This expression comes to us from card games. In some games a marker, called the "buck," is kept in front of the dealer to remind the players where the deal belongs. Thus, when the buck is passed, the responsibility for the deal moves on. From this we get "passing the buck"—shifting responsibility to someone else.

Why does the nursery rhyme "Pat-a-cake, pat-a-cake, Baker's man" say, "Mark it with a T"?

In case you have forgotten it, the rhyme goes like this:

> Pat-a-cake, pat-a-cake, baker's man!
> So I will, master, as fast as I can:
> Pat it, and prick it, and mark it with T,
> Put it in the oven for Tommy and me.

This nursery rhyme is over 350 years old, and has appeared in various forms. Most people assume that the *T* is for Tommy. Not so; in fact, Tommy doesn't appear at all in many versions. The *T* was actually intended to be a cross. It was customary in the Middle Ages to mark various baked goods with the sign of the cross. The custom survives even today in hot cross buns.

Why do we call it a "sandwich"?

John Montagu (1718–1792), the fourth Earl of Sandwich, was a compulsive gambler who refused to leave the card table for a meal. Instead, he would request a servant to bring him a slice of meat between two pieces of bread. It caught on, and everybody was eating sandwiches.

Why do we say "pay through the nose"?

The most likely explanation is that the expression refers to the head tax imposed on Ireland by the Danes in the ninth century. Those who didn't pay were punished by having their noses slit, leading to the name "nose tax," which later may have suggested "paying through the nose."

Why is payoff money called "payola"?

This very specific term refers to money paid to disc jockeys for playing and promoting a recording. From the 1930s on, it was a common term within the music industry. In 1959 Burton Lane, president of the American Guild of Authors and Composers, released a letter to the press in which he described large-scale bribery of this sort. The letter used the word "payola," which, in the ensuing scandal, came into widespread use.

Why do we say "peeping Tom"?

Any person who spies on others—for example, someone who peeks at night into a house—is called a "peeping Tom." The phrase goes back to the legend of Lady Godiva. Her husband, the Lord of Coventry, levied high tolls on his subjects. A kind-hearted woman, she appealed to him so often to abolish these taxes that he agreed to do so if she would ride naked through the village. Deciding to call his bluff, she sent out a proclamation asking the townspeople to stay indoors behind closed shutters while she rode. Everyone did, except Tom the Tailor, who peeped through a hole in his shutter. According to the legend, he was immediately stricken blind. Lady Godiva's husband kept his promise and abolished the tolls, but "peeping Tom" came into the language to memorialize the foolish tailor.

Why do we say "pin money"?

At one time pins were manufactured under a monopoly granted by the Crown, and were thus very expensive. This phrase, which is several centuries old, originally referred to money put aside specifically to buy pins. But it has come to mean any small fund over which the wife—the person who would usually buy pins—has control.

Why do we say "pleased as Punch"?

The "Punch" in question is the clown in the old puppet shows, Punch and Judy. These shows were popular from the seventeenth century until the rise of modern entertainment, and were often a feature at English fairs. At the end of the show Punch always lorded it over his difficult wife, Judy, and was obviously pleased with his triumph. "Pleased as Punch" thus describes someone who is conspicuously happy about something, especially an achievement or triumph.

Why do we say "run the gauntlet"?

To "run the gauntlet" is to undergo an ordeal. The original running of the gauntlet was in fact an ordeal. It consisted of having a convicted man strip to the waist and run between two lines of his peers, who struck him with rods or whips as he passed by. The British, who practiced this form of punishment during the Thirty Years' War, were said to have learned it from the Swedes. They also borrowed the word for it from the Swedes, who called it the *gatloppe,* or "running of the lane." In England that word was corrupted into "gantlope" and then "gantlet," which finally became "gauntlet."

Why is one who takes the blame called a "scapegoat"?

Originally this word represented just what it seems to mean— an "escape goat." On the Day of Atonement the Jews would bring two goats to the altar. The high priest chose one to be sacrificed. Then he confessed the sins of the congregation over the head of the second. After that, the goat was taken to the edge of the village and allowed to escape into the wilderness, taking all the people's sins with it. That was the first "scapegoat." Now the word describes a person who, like that ancient goat, is blamed for other people's mistakes or crimes.

Why is gossip called "scuttlebutt"?

The original "scuttlebutt" was a shipboard cask which contained the crew's drinking water. Apparently what happened there was just about the same as what happens today around office drinking fountains—people gathered to exchange gossip.

Why do we say "posh"?

Anything posh is fashionable and exclusive. The most expensive accommodations on a luxury liner—which is where the word actually originated—are very posh. When a ship traveled from England to India, the port side of the ship was shady, and therefore the most desirable and expensive. On the homeward journey the starboard side was shady. Thus, the most desirable staterooms were *P*ort *O*ut, *S*tarboard *H*ome.

Why do we say "read the riot act"?

There have been numerous laws designed to keep the peace. The Riot Act passed by the British Parliament in 1714 was the first really comprehensive law of this sort. It contained an order to disperse, and was to be read by officials to any unruly crowd of twelve or more people. From this, "reading the riot act" has taken on the less literal meaning of strongly reprimanding someone.

Why do we say "the real McCoy"?

"Kid" McCoy was a well-known prizefighter of the 1890s. One night a barroom heckler dared him to a fight, and kept saying that if he were really "Kid" McCoy he'd do it. Finally McCoy gave in and instantly flattened the man. When the heckler came to, the first thing he said was, "That's the real McCoy, all right." This was the origin of this popular expression used to refer to the genuine article, the real thing.

Why would anyone keep "a skeleton in the closet"?

Years ago, it was against the law for a doctor to dissect a body unless it was that of a dead criminal. However, there just weren't enough such bodies to supply medical researchers in those days. As a result, many doctors became grave robbers. But since grave robbing was also against the law, the stolen bodies had to be concealed. Where, in a doctor's office, can you hide a skeleton? Why, in the closet, of course! Eventually the public image evolved of every doctor having a skeleton in his closet, and from that the expression expanded to include anyone who conceals some shady or disreputable fact about himself.

Why do we say "put your shoulder to the wheel"?

This odd expression is actually a very logical way of referring to old-fashioned hard work. It dates back to America's frontier days, when wagon trains heading west often got stuck in the mud of those unpaved wagon trails. When that happened, the men would get out and, while the horses pulled up front, would push the wagon from the back—by putting their shoulders to the wheel. A covered wagon loaded with all a family's worldly goods was very heavy; needless to say, "putting your shoulder to the wheel" was hard work!

Why do we say "rule of thumb"?

Centuries ago, carpenters and tailors regarded a thumb's breadth as equal to one inch. Likewise, to regulate the fermentation, brewers determined the heat of brewing liquor by dipping their thumbs into the vat. Today the term "rule of thumb" has been extended to mean any principle based on practice and experience as opposed to knowledge from scientific experimentation or formal instruction.

Why do we say "shoot the bull"?

To "shoot the bull" is to talk at random and informally about any number of subjects. The expression originated in the barnyard where cows and bulls were kept. Young men wishing to talk among themselves might step over the fence into the barnyard. Such gatherings were, of course, called "bull sessions."

Why do we call it a "slush fund"?

In the British Navy it was once customary to collect the grease— or "slush"—from the cook's galley to lubricate the masts. Whatever was left over was sold, and the money put into a fund for the enlisted men. Nowadays a "slush fund" can be any fund with an undesignated purpose.

Why do we speak of being "sold down the river"?

To be "sold down the river" is to be betrayed or deceived. The expression grew up during the domestic slave trade of the early nineteenth century. Southern plantations were expanding, but it was illegal to import slaves after 1808. So they were purchased from the exhausted tobacco belt area of the upper South and brought down the Mississippi to the slave markets of Natchez and New Orleans. To be "sold down the river" meant losing home and family—the ultimate betrayal.

Why do we use the phrase "sour grapes"?

The reference is to one of Aesop's fables, "The Fox and the Grapes." In this story a fox saw mouth-watering grapes hanging

from a vine. As it was a hot day, he wanted them very much and leaped for them. Time after time he jumped, getting hotter and thirstier by the minute; but try as he might, he could not reach them. Finally he rationalized that it was a good thing they were out of reach—they looked sour anyway! Today, when we find something desirable out of reach, we may use the fox's rationalization. And that's "sour grapes."

Why are left-handed baseball pitchers called "southpaws"?

Most baseball diamonds are laid out so that the batter will not be looking west (into the sun) but east. As the pitcher faces the batter, his left hand is toward the south. A ball thrown by a southpaw is harder to hit because of its curve. It is also harder to catch. For this reason, while left-handed pitchers are valued, southpaw shortstops, second basemen or third basemen are rarely used.

Why do we "talk turkey"?

To sit down and negotiate a good deal is often referred to as "talking turkey." This expression first appeared when the Pilgrims traded with the Indians—perhaps a nice necklace for a turkey (it seems as though the white man always wanted a turkey from the red man). Soon the Indian would grunt, "You come to 'talk turkey'?"

Why do we say "sow wild oats"?

In the British Isles the wild oat—which resembles the cultivated oat—is a common weed. English farmers used "sowing wild oats" to mean that a person was sowing worthless seed. The phrase then came to be used figuratively, in the sense that a youth spent in dissipation leads to a worthless harvest.

Why do we say "call a spade a spade"?

In the first century A.D. the Greek biographer Plutarch used this expression—at least that's how what he wrote was translated. The catch is that the Greek word for "spade" was very similar to the word for "boat." So the original may have really been "call a boat a boat."

Why do we call revealing a secret "spilling the beans"?

The "beans" in question go back to the ancient Greeks, who used them as a method of voting on new candidates for their exclusive clubs. Each member had two beans, and could put either one in the jar; the white bean was a "yes" vote, and the brown bean was a "no." The beans were counted in strict secrecy, so that a prospective member would never know how many people voted against him. Obviously, a high percentage of brown beans would be a real embarrassment. But occasionally a clumsy member would accidentally knock over the jar, and the secret was out. He had spilled the beans!

Why do we use the terms "starboard" and "port"?

If you face forward on a ship, "starboard" is on your right. Anglo-Saxon vessels were steered with an oar held on that side. *Ster* meant rudder, and *bord* meant the side of a boat. So the rudder side was the *sterbord*. It may be that "port" was adopted for the left side because boats were anchored at harbor with the steering oar away from the dock and the left side against the wharf, or facing port. Incidentally, "bord" (side) also shows up in "man overboard."

Why do we speak of "stealing thunder"?

This expression originated in the early eighteenth century with the English dramatist John Dennis. For the production of his play *Appius and Virginia* in London's Drury Lane Theater, he invented an improved method of simulating thunder. The play itself failed, and the manager withdrew it, much to the author's disgust. Not long after, Dennis went to the Drury Lane Theater to see *Macbeth* and heard his new method of producing thunder employed. Furious, he cried: "The villains will not play my play but they rattle my thunder."

Why do we say "stone broke"?

While "stone broke" is how we describe an individual who is suffering from severe financial hardship, it is interesting to note that being "stone broke" was originally a result of poverty. The expression refers to the custom of breaking a craftman's stone bench when he failed to pay his debts.

Why is an informer called a "stool pigeon"?

When a person squeals on somebody, he or she is often referred to as a "stool pigeon." It may be said that this expression is, in truth, for the birds, because it originates from the old practice of tying pigeons to a stool, or perch, to lure other pigeons into the hunters' snares.

Why do we say "straight from the horse's mouth"?

This means to have information from the person who is in the

best position to know. It refers to the fact that you don't have to believe what anybody tells you about a horse's age—you can look in the mouth. In the horse's lower jaw, the first two permanent teeth do not appear until the horse is two and a half years old. The next pair appears a year later, and the third set after another year. Thus, a young racer's age can be accurately determined by examining the mouth.

Why is a naive person called a "sucker"?

The comparison here is to any young animal who is not yet weaned. Someone who is easily deceived or gullible is said to be, like this infant, a "sucker," although certainly one does not have a helpless newborn animal in mind when such name-calling is used. The term implies that the sucker is not only gullible but stupid as well!

Why do we refer to unwanted items as "white elephants"?

A white elephant is an Indian elephant of a pale-gray or yellowish color. Such animals have been considered sacred in many countries, including Siam. A popular explanation of the phrase "a white elephant," meaning something that is ruinously expensive to maintain, is that the King of Siam would give such an animal to a nobleman he wished to bring down. The nobleman would, of course, have to maintain the animal in style, and would go broke in the process. There is, however, no evidence to support this theory. In fact, only the King was considered worthy of owning a white elephant, so all such animals were brought to him alone. The animals were kept in special stables, their only value being their significance as a symbol of royal dignity. That these useless animals should be so expensively maintained led to the phrase "a white elephant."

Why is a final work called a "swan song"?

This phrase comes from the romantic old legend that a swan sings one beautiful song before it dies. In fact, swans never sing. Nevertheless, we use this phrase to refer to the last work of a great artist.

Why do we say "take for a ride"?

To be "taken for a ride" may be a joke—a matter of being kidded about something. It may also mean being deluded and cheated by someone. Its original meaning was more sinister. The expression arose after World War I during a wave of gang warfare. A man who made an enemy of a gang leader might be invited for a ride in the leader's car to try to settle their differences. But it was a ride from which he might not return.

Why do we speak of the "third degree"?

When we talk of getting the "third degree," we are referring to persistent and detailed questioning. More specifically, the term is applied to illegal police methods, and was first so used in 1911 by Major Richard Sylvester, a Washington, D.C., superintendent of police. "Third degree" in this context means subjecting a prisoner to physical or mental torture to elicit information or a confession. Traditional third-degree methods included beating the prisoner with a rubber hose, which leaves no marks, or subjecting him to continuous questioning for several days. The Supreme Court has ruled that confessions obtained by such third-degree methods are illegal under the Seventh Amendment, which bars "cruel and unusual punishment." It is thought that Major Sylvester borrowed the term from the brotherhood of Masons. The third degree of advancement in Masonry is Master Mason, which is said to have an unusually elaborate initiation ceremony.

Why is a drunk described as being "three sheets in the wind"?

This term arose in the early nineteenth century among English sailors. The "sheets" in question are not sails, but chains that regulate the angle of the sails. If these sheets are loose, the ship will be as unstable on the water as a thoroughly drunk man is on his feet.

Why do we say "throw in the towel"?

This term, which means "surrender," comes from the boxing ring. When a fighter is being badly beaten, his manager can stop the fight and concede by throwing a towel into the ring. The towel is used simply because it is sure to be kept nearby to dry off a fighter's perspiration between rounds.

Why do we speak of "throwing one's hat in the ring"?

When a man throws his hat in the ring, he is announcing his candidacy for office. The phrase comes to us from the world of wrestling and boxing, where an item of clothing could be thrown down to show a man's willingness to fight. Miners in Cornwall, England, still challenge each other to wrestling matches by throwing their hats on the ground. In the same way, an American lumberjack may start a fight by throwing down some article of clothing as a dare. In the early nineteenth century it was a custom in the American West for a man to express his readiness to wrestle or box by actually throwing his hat in the ring. Theodore Roosevelt, a sportsman, was the first person known to use the phrase in a political sense. In 1912, asked whether he intended to run for President again, he replied to the reporters: "My hat is in the ring."

Why was the Model T called the "Tin Lizzie"?

Introduced in 1908, the Model T (which was simply the design that followed the Model S) was produced until 1927, for a total of over fifteen million Model T's. The car was so popular that the Ford Motor Company periodically had to refuse orders in order to catch up on its backlog.

The Model T was not made of tin but of sheet metal; it was initially called "the tin car" only because it was built for the masses, as other Fords had been. Why "Lizzie"? In those days many families employed a domestic servant, who might typically be named Lizzie. Like her, the Model T helped do everything six days a week, then got prettied up on Sunday and took off. In time, the "tin car" came to be compared to the family domestic—thus, the "Tin Lizzie."

Why do we say "two shakes of a lamb's tail"?

This is probably an embroidery upon an older saying that meant the same thing, "in a couple of shakes." That saying could have referred to anything that could be shaken quickly—dice or a cloth, for instance. Someone added to it, having noticed how quickly a lamb shakes its tail, and now anything that takes very little time is described as being done in "two shakes of a lamb's tail."

Why do we say "up to snuff"?

An item is "up to snuff" when it is of the usual high quality. Earlier in the century, "up to snuff" referred to a person who was alert and well informed. The word "snuff" in the phrase is closely related to "sniff," which can be used to mean "smell," in the sense of the old phrase "to sniff danger." A person who was "up to snuff" was on his toes and able to follow a scent or clue.

Why do we call them "free-lancers"?

It's been said that a "free-lancer" is any newspaperman who's out of work! The "free-lances" of the Middle Ages, however, really carried lances. They were professional soldiers—sometimes led by a knight—who hired out as mercenaries to feudal lords. They were first described as free-lancers around 1820. Since that time the term has broadened to include any person who sells his services without a long-term commitment.

Why is a V-shaped hairline called a "widow's peak"?

From the time of the Roman emperors until 1498, white was worn for mourning. That year, Anne of Brittany chose black for mourning when her husband, Charles VIII, died. She was so attractive in her black costume that eventually Louis XII of France married her. To go with the newly popular black mourning costumes, designers created a V-shaped bonnet. When hair grows naturally in that shape, it is called a "widow's peak" after this style. The ancient superstition holds that a woman whose hair grows like this will be widowed young—but will remarry soon, as Anne of Brittany did.

Why is a rooftop platform called a "widow's walk"?

The popular myth is that sailors' wives climbed onto these platforms to watch for ships. But you will find such platforms far from the sea. They arose out of the need to fight chimney fires. When chimneys were in the middle of a house, quick access was vital in case of a fire, and such fires were common. Roofs had an opening with a lid, called a roof scuttle, and the platforms were developed for safety reasons.

Why do we say "a wolf in sheep's clothing"?

In this expression the term "wolf" means a man who avidly
pursues women. The phrase comes from a fable by Aesop. Such
men, he said, are like the wolf who enters the fold wrapped in a
sheepskin. By appearing to be a harmless sheep, the wolf could
capture the young lambs.

Why is the "guillotine" so called?

It is commonly supposed that the guillotine was named after its
inventor, but that is not the case. It wasn't even called a guillotine
when it was first used in France. The instrument was an adaptation
of an Italian device and was named the "Louison" after its adaptor,
a Dr. Louis. Dr. Joseph Guillotin's contribution was to help push
through the French National Assembly in 1792 a resolution
adopting the guillotine as the official means of execution. He
meant well, as it was quicker and more humane than the existing
methods. First used to execute criminals, the machine became a
political weapon during the Reign of Terror, when 8,000
Frenchmen died under its blade. Dr. Guillotin's family resented
so strongly having their name attached to this instrument of
terror that they officially changed the family name when he died.

Why is a very short haircut called a "crew cut"?

The "crew cut" is so named because oarsmen commonly wore this
cool and trouble-free hairstyle. The very short haircut has also
had other names. Since it was the favored style of Von Hindenburg,
President of Germany from 1925 to 1932, it was known as a
"Hindenburg haircut." Later, it was called a "military cut." But
before that time, anyone who wanted such a style went to a livery
stable. There, using a horse clipper, the stableman would give a
"pig shave cut." In the 1950s the cut came to be called a "flattop"
and a "brush cut," both names reflecting its appearance.

Why is going to prison referred to as being sent "up the river"?

This was originally an underworld term referring to a sentence in jail. The reference is probably to Sing Sing, the famous prison which lies "up the river" from New York City.

Why is it called a "dandelion"?

The origin of "dandelion" is the French *"dent de lion,"* or "lion's tooth." The plant's jagged leaves do in fact resemble the teeth of a lion, and several other European languages refer to the plant as "lion's tooth."

Why are fists called "dukes"?

The slang term "dukes," meaning fists, has an odd origin. The Duke of Wellington had such a large nose that "duke" became a synonym for "nose." Then, so the theory goes, a man's fist became a "duke buster." In time this was shortened, and fists were simply called "dukes." "Put up your dukes" has long been a familiar expression meaning "Get ready to fight!"

Why is the breakfast dish called "eggs Benedict"?

Samuel Benedict, a prominent New Yorker, is credited with this famous high-calorie breakfast dish. One morning at the old Waldorf-Astoria Hotel, he ordered poached eggs, bacon, and toast with hollandaise sauce. Oscar, the maître d', suggested substituting a muffin and a slice of ham for the toast and bacon. Benedict was pleased with the results, as was Oscar, who christened it "eggs Benedict" and added it to the menu.

Why do we observe weddings as we do?

Many wedding customs are relics of earlier forms of marriage. The first such form was marriage by capture. Primitive man would simply seize his mate and carry her off by force. At the same time he would be defended by his "best man," a friend who would accompany him to ward off attacks by the girl's kinsmen while he was abducting her. The "honeymoon" was the period of time he hid her until her clan gave up searching for her. The word "wedding" itself comes from the second stage, marriage by barter. The "wed" was the money or livestock the Anglo-Saxon groom gave to the bride's father. The custom of the father "giving" away the bride also goes back to this form of marriage. While marriage is now a contract of mutual affection, our wedding customs show that this was not always the case.

Why are Northerners called "Damned Yankees"?

It seems logical to assume that this term was invented by Southerners during the Civil War. But the fact is that the term was first used by the "Yorkers" in the Continental Army during the Revolutionary War. They applied it to the "provincials," or country boys. But as hostilities increased between the North and South, it was natural for Southerners to adopt and use the term.

Why is something of immense size referred to as "gargantuan"?

The word "gargantuan" derives from the name Gargantua, a friendly giant with a huge appetite, who first appeared in medieval folktales. In 1534 the French writer Rabelais used the character in a satire entitled *The Horrific Life of the Great Gargantua*. Although peaceful enough, the hero was gigantic in size and had an appetite to match. His favorite first course, for instance, was six pilgrims!

Why do we call enthusiasts "fans"?

"Fan," meaning a devoted admirer of a sport, athletic team, famous person, etc., is a contraction of "fanatic." The word seems to have originated in the 1880s when Chris Van der Ahe, owner of the St. Louis Browns, referred to Charles Haas as a baseball fanatic. Sportswriters found the word appealing and began to call all baseball followers "fanatics." The headline writers shortened the word, for convenience, to "fans." The term was so useful that it was applied to ardent enthusiasts in other sports and the entertainment field.

Why are they called "French fries"?

It seems odd to many people that the only place in France where you can get "French fries" is at an American hamburger stand. Actually, however, the origin of this popular food is probably British. In England, fried potatoes are served with fish and are called "chips." The American name, "French fries," reflects the method of preparation. Any meat or vegetable which is cut into narrow strips before cooking is said to be "Frenched." So Frenched and fried potatoes have become simply "French fries."

Why are first- and second-year students called, respectively, "freshmen" and "sophomores"?

The word "freshman" goes back to 1550, and its origin is obvious; a first-year student then, as now, was *fresh*—untried and inexperienced. And he was a *man;* college in those days was definitely not for women. Because of this origin, many feminists prefer "first-year student" or even "freshperson." "Sophomore" is equally interesting in its origin. The Greek *sophos* meant "wise," and *moros* meant "foolish." It is well known, or assumed at least, that sophomores are given to making confident pronouncements on weighty issues, while in fact they are quite immature and relatively unlearned.

Why is it called a "funny bone"?

If a nerve is pressed at a specific point in the elbow, a painful, tingling sensation results. Why, then, is it called the "funny bone"? One reasonable conjecture is that it is a play on the Latin word *humerus,* which is the medical name of the long bone in the upper arm.

Why do we say "worth his salt"?

This expression only goes back to the nineteenth century, but the reference is to the ancient Romans. Part of a Roman soldier's pay was a "salarium," an allowance for buying salt. The mineral was not so easy to get then as it is now, and was known to be necessary for health. So a soldier who earned his pay was "worth his salt."

Why is a group of affiliated companies called a "conglomerate"?

In geology, the term "conglomerate" means a rock composed of pebbles and gravel embedded in some kind of cementing material. A group of companies that constitute a single corporation is accordingly called a conglomerate.

Why is it called "ghost writing"?

You can't see a ghost. You can't see a ghost writer either, in a manner of speaking. He is the actual but unacknowledged author of a book, article, or speech for which someone else takes the credit.

Why is it called "Gothic" architecture?

Not because of the Goths. They had nothing to do with this form of architecture. And in fact, the architecture of the Middle Ages was not called Gothic until the Renaissance, when painters and writers began to use the term as a way of expressing contempt for such architecture, which they thought barbaric.

Why are whole-wheat crackers called "graham crackers"?

Food faddism is not just a product of the modern age. In the 1830s a Presbyterian minister named Sylvester Graham was an ardent advocate of temperance. He believed that not only must man abstain from drink, but that it was necessary to undo the effects of intemperance with a whole-grain vegetarian diet. Meat, he claimed, led to sexual excess, and mustard and ketchup brought on insanity. Graham also urged the substitution of whole-wheat bread for white. Graham food stores, much like today's health food stores, sprang up everywhere, and were violently opposed by butchers and bakers. Like all fads, this one soon came to an end. But modern science has proved Graham right in some respects. Americans do eat far too much meat, and the refining of flour does rob it of nutrients. Graham's followers called their whole-wheat flour "graham flour"; and crackers made from it were "graham crackers," as they are today.

Why is a football field called a "gridiron"?

A gridiron is a flat framework of parallel metal bars which can be placed over a flame for broiling food. A football field, with its rectangular shape and parallel white lines, resembles this device. The famous Gridiron Club in Washington, D.C., is so named because at dinners the members satirize—that is, put over a flame, or "broil"—important public figures.

Why is a married man called a "husband"?

This word comes from several sources which combine to mean "one who manages a household." The Anglo-Saxon word *hus* means "house." The old Norse *bondi* means "freeholder" and comes from *bua,* meaning "to dwell." Over time the word came to be used to refer to a married man, who was regarded as manager of the household. The word is still used, in its original sense of a household manager, to refer to the shipboard officer responsible for taking on supplies before his ship sails. The original meaning of the word is also inherent in the phrase "husband one's resources," meaning "use them economically."

Why is the color called "khaki"?

The word derives from the Persian *khak,* meaning "earth" or "dust." It entered the language by way of the British occupation of India. The first British troops in that country wore regulation red or white uniforms—very conspicuous in the dry season, when dust turned everything brown. Since the bright colors made them perfect targets for snipers, the troops learned to dip their uniforms in muddy streams. This early form of camouflage resulted in the switch to khaki—or earth-colored—uniforms, first in India, later worldwide.

Why does "KP" mean cleaning the mess hall?

Kitchen police, or KPs, are enlisted men assigned to work in the kitchen. While KP duty has always been dreaded, the term itself seems to have been around only since about 1930. To "police," meaning to keep an area neat and orderly, is an older term, going back to the turn of the century. At that time a familiar saying on army posts went: "If it's small enough, pick it up; if not, paint it; if it moves, salute it." In KP, you clean it!

Why do we use the term "lunatic"?

Luna means "moon," and *tic* means "struck"—so a "lunatic" is "moonstruck." Primitive people believed the full moon affected the mind. Sleeping in its light could cause mental defectiveness, and looking directly at the full moon could bring on insanity. There is no evidence to support this belief, but it is true that even today many fire departments dread the full moon. Although psychiatrists find it difficult to explain, pyromaniacs are often stirred into action during the full moon, and more fires occur then.

Why do we believe groundhogs predict the weather?

This tradition originated in Europe, but there the hedgehog was the forecaster. The closest thing the Pilgrims could find to a hedgehog was the groundhog. The belief is that the animal comes out of hibernation on February 2, Candlemas Day, and looks around him. If the day is sunny and he can see his shadow, he goes back into his burrow, anticipating six more weeks of bad weather. But if he can't see his shadow, he believes that winter is over. The fact is, in northern climates February 2 is generally far too early for the groundhog to come out. If it should, however, it invariably goes back in, whether it sees its shadow or not.

Why are they called "leotards"?

Leotards owe their popularity to a nineteenth-century French trapeze artist who wore the tight-fitting elastic garments for the torso and advocated them for men, as "a more natural garb which does not hide your best features." His name? Jules Léotard. Today, women wear leotards more frequently than men—indicating, perhaps, that they, more than men, like to wear a more natural garb which does not hide their best features.

Why are naval cadets called "midshipmen"?

Young men in the British Navy who were training to become officers were always quartered on the lower deck—amidships. Thus, cadets and low-ranking officers came to be called "midshipmen," the term still used at Annapolis.

Why do we call the record of a meeting the "minutes"?

"Minutes" of a meeting have nothing to do with time. The word stems from the Latin *minutus,* or "small." Records of meetings have always been written in miniature, or shorthand, and transcribed later.

Why is it called a "monkey wrench"?

Tradition has it that wrenches with adjustable moving jaws were invented by Charles Moncke, a London blacksmith. Since "Moncke" is pronounced almost like "monkey," the name of the tool changed easily from "Moncke wrench" to "monkey wrench."

Why is it called a "kangaroo court"?

A "kangaroo court" is a mock court set up outside of established legal procedures. Institutions of this sort exist in most large prisons, where inmates fine and punish other inmates for various "infractions." The most plausible theory claims that the phrase originated in Australia, which at one time was a penal colony of the British Empire. There, the irregular proceedings of such unauthorized courts were compared to the erratic leaps of the kangaroo.

Why do we call side whiskers "sideburns"?

The original name was "burnsides," after Ambrose E. Burnside, a Civil War general who wore long side whiskers with a shaved chin. Because whiskers are on the sides of the face, the syllables were soon transposed into "sideburns."

Why do we say "ornery"?

"Ornery," meaning stubborn and of an ugly disposition, is a corruption of "ordinary." The word came to the American colonies chiefly by way of the Scotch-Irish immigrants. Since most of those immigrants settled in the West and South, the word "ornery" is more commonly found in those regions.

Why do we call cents "pennies"?

There has never been an official "penny" in the United States. The Congressional act creating this coin refers to it as a cent, a name which comes from the Latin *centum,* or "hundred." But the English penny was widely used here until a law in 1787 banned all foreign currency from circulation. Thereafter the cent took on the name "penny." Because it was the old English currency, the word "penny" appears in a number of old sayings, such as "A penny for your thoughts" and "Penny wise and pound foolish." The word "penny" itself probably comes from the Latin *pannus,* or "cloth"; in barbarian Europe, pieces of cloth were used as a means of exchange.

Why do we call it a "pineapple"?

A pineapple, surprisingly enough, is not the single fruit it appears to be in the supermarket, but a group of small fruits clustered tightly around a central core, or stem. The whole thing rather resembles a pinecone, for which reason it was named a "pineapple."

Why is the hairstyle called a "pompadour"?

It was so named because a beautiful mistress of Louis XV, Madame de Pompadour, wore her golden hair swept straight up from the forehead. She is believed to have had such beauty and intellectual charm that the king gave her a room in the palace itself. Although she died young, in her early forties, the Marquise de Pompadour's then unusual hairstyle became a household word which has long outlived her otherwise illustrious reputation.

Why is it called a "round robin"?

A "round robin" is a tournament in which each contestant plays every other contestant. Its name has nothing to do with the bird, but comes from *ruban,* French for "ribbon." The first round robin was devised in eighteenth-century France, where the king, if angered by a petition, was likely to have the first signer beheaded. Naturally, nobody wanted to be first. Finally someone came up with the idea of having all the petitioners sign a ribbon and then joining the ribbon in a circle. Thus, nobody's name was first on the list! A similar device originated in the British Navy, where the ship's captain could order hanged the first signer of a petition of grievance, who was assumed to be the leader. There, the signatures of the petitioners were arranged in a circle, like the spokes of a ship's wheel.

Why are criminals called "thugs"?

Until the mid-nineteenth century, a group of religious assassins called Thugs terrorized India. As part of their duty to Kali Ma, goddess of destruction, they robbed and murdered unwary travelers. Sometimes they merely followed the victim; often they became friendly fellow travelers, accompanying the victim until the right opportunity arose. After the murder, which was most often done by strangulation, the Thugs would perform religious rites over the body and bury it. Part of the plunder belonged to the assassins, and part was sacrificed to Kali. A well-organized sect, the Thugs had secret languages, both spoken and sign, by which they identified one another. Our use of the word "thug" to mean any gangster or criminal is borrowed from this now extinct sect.

Why is the Pope's official residence called the "Vatican"?

The west bank of the Tiber, near the present Vatican, was once the site of an Etruscan settlement called *Vaticum*. While it is not known for certain how the town got its name, *vates* means *"prophet"* in Latin. It may be that a priest revealed his prophecies on this site. Over time, the word "Vatican" was applied to the hill on which Vatican City now stands, rather than to the low land near the river.

Why do we speak of a "fourflusher"?

A "fourflusher" is a faker, or bluffer. The name comes to us from the game of poker, in which five cards of the same suit constitute a flush. A hand with four cards of one suit and one card of another is a four flush, and is worthless. A player may, however, bluff and bet as if he has a full flush, hoping to deceive his opponents. Such a player is, literally, a "fourflusher."

Why do we measure firewood in "cords"?

The word "cord" itself means a "small rope of twisted strands." A "cord of wood" is a stack measuring four feet high, four feet wide, and eight feet long, totaling 128 cubic feet. Why is that cubic area called a cord? Originally, stacks of firewood were measured with a

cord of a specific length. Although that is no longer done, we still
refer to a "cord of wood."

Why do sportsmen not have to fear "heavy air"?

Many golfers and baseball fans believe that when the air is damp
it is "heavy," and puts enough drag on a ball to shorten the
distance it travels. Air does have weight, it is true, but water vapor
is actually lighter than air, not heavier. So "heaviness" of the air
doesn't ruin a shot. It is true, however, that moisture on the club
or bat may cause the grip to be insecure and the shot, therefore,
less powerful.

Why is the harvest moon so bright?

The usefulness of the harvest moon led primitive people to believe
it was a gift of the gods. Shining as it does at the time of the
autumn equinox, between September 15th and 20th, it allowed
them to harvest by moonlight. The reason the harvest moon seems
brighter is that the oblique direction of its path makes a smaller
angle with the horizon at this time of year. The next full moon is
called the hunter's moon because farmers, their work done, can
then go hunting.

Why are we told not to eat green apples?

Most people believe that unripe apples will give you a stomachache. It probably follows from the widespread belief that what
tastes bad is bad for you. However, as we all know, what tastes
good isn't necessarily good for you either. Junk food is a case in
point. As for apples, according to medical authorities, an apple
that is eaten slowly and thoroughly chewed can't hurt you—green
or ripe.

Why do we use the term "bench mark"?

You might suppose that the first "bench mark" was a line on a carpenter's bench for purposes of measuring. In fact, the phrase was originally a surveyor's term, referring to any permanent part of the landscape, such as a rock outcropping. A "bench mark" has a known position and known altitude, and can therefore be used as a reference point to determine other altitudes. The term is now used figuratively to mean a high standard for achievement.

Why is a front-button sweater called a "cardigan"?

During the Crimean War, Britain's Lord Cardigan was brigadier-general in command of the Light Brigade. He distinguished himself greatly by his courage in the Battle of Balaclava, in what became known as "The Charge of the Light Brigade." When he returned home he was cheered for his heroism and invited to stay at Windsor Castle. The woolen jacket he had worn during the campaign was named a "cardigan" and became widely popular.

Why is breakfast food called "cereal"?

This everyday word comes from Roman mythology. The goddess Ceres ruled over grain, the harvest, and all agriculture. She assumed an important role during the great drought of 496 B.C. Because they believed she had answered their prayers for rain, the Romans built numerous temples to her and established annual festivals in her honor. The grain markets were controlled by the guardians of the temples, and grain was known as *cerealis,* "of Ceres." Our word "cereal" includes all edible grains, but is more commonly used to refer to the breakfast food.

Why do we believe baseball originated in America?

There has always been a strong desire to believe the national game was invented here, but there is some evidence to the contrary. This subject was so hotly debated early in the century that in 1907 a commission was formed to settle the question. It reported that Abner Doubleday had invented the game in 1839, and that it was entirely unrelated to foreign games. Since that time, however, much has been published linking baseball with British games. As a matter of fact, one game was even called "baseball." Eighteenth-century illustrations survive showing a batter at a plate, a catcher, a pitcher, and two bases. In the early nineteenth century the English played another game called "rounders." The game was played on a diamond with four bases, and featured fouls, strike-outs and home runs. One difference was that the runner in rounders was put out by being hit by the ball. It is interesting to note, however, that that is the way Doubleday himself taught the game!

Why is it called "moonshine"?

"Moonshine" is generally associated with homemade stills in the mountain districts of Kentucky, Tennessee, Virginia and North Carolina. Many people think the whiskey from these stills was called "moonshine" because it had to be made at night to evade revenue officers. Actually, the term may not be American at all. In an English dictionary dated 1785, "moonshine" is defined as white brandy smuggled into England by night.

Why is the cocktail called a "manhattan"?

The "manhattan," a potent cocktail made of whiskey and vermouth, was invented in the 1870s. It is named after its birthplace, a men's social club in New York City called the Manhattan Club.

Why do we use the term "lame duck"?

A "lame duck" is an officeholder who has lost the election for the next term but still has some time to serve before his successor is inaugurated. The term comes to us from Exchange Alley— eighteenth-century London's equivalent of Wall Street. There, people who couldn't pay their debts were referred to as "lame ducks" because, it was said, they "waddled out of the Alley."

Why do we use the word "landlubber"?

Most people think a "landlubber" is a land-lover who doesn't like ships. Actually, it is entirely possible for a "landlubber" to love the sea. The word really derives not from *lover* but from the old Anglo-Saxon *lobbe*—a "clumsy novice." A "landlubber" is someone who is so awkward aboard ship that it is assumed he'd be awkward on land as well.

Why is it called "logrolling"?

When legislators support each other's pet projects, it is called "logrolling." This picturesque phrase goes back to the days of the Western migration. A settler would ask his new neighbors for help in clearing his land—rolling away the heavy logs. In turn, he would agree to lend a hand with any project on which they might need help.

Why do we say "man and wife"?

It would seem that this phrase should either be "husband and wife" or "man and woman." In fact, this form has been with us since the Norman conquest, when "man" meant "husband," as it does in Scotland to this day.

Why do we call hypnotism "mesmerism"?

Oddly enough, Franz Anton Mesmer (1734–1815), who first used hypnotism, never realized what he was doing. This highly educated man first experimented with magnets, and found he could cure diseases ranging from stomachache to paralysis. But in further experiments he discovered that the cures occurred whether or not he held a magnet. His new power, "animal magnetism," became the rage of Paris. In seance-like settings patients would sit together listening to soft music. After an hour or so Mesmer would talk to each patient and stroke him with a little wand. The object was to produce a "crisis"—trembling, convulsions, fainting, even dancing—and it worked. At the height of his popularity, Mesmer was discredited by a commission appointed by France's Louis XVI, whose members included Benjamin Franklin. It was left to one of Mesmer's pupils to identify what his teacher had really done and call it "mesmerism."

Why do we say "O.K."?

One common explanation of the origin of "O.K." is that Andrew Jackson wrote it on legal papers to stand for "orl korrect." But no documents with this mark in his handwriting have ever been found. A more likely explanation is that the term was first used by the Democratic O.K. Club during the second presidential campaign of Martin Van Buren. Van Buren, who came from the village of Kinderhook, New York, had been given the nickname "Old Kinderhook," and that was what the letters "O.K." stood for.

Index

A

Academy of Motion Picture Arts and Sciences, 109
According to Hoyle, 59
Ace in the hole, 60-61
Achilles' heel, 61
Actor, as ham, 95
Addison, Joseph, 106
Agassiz, Louis, 14
Air
 heavy, 143
 at night, as bad for you, 18-19
Air pocket, 26
Alger, Horatio, wealth of heroes, 49-50
All that glitters is not gold, 52
An ax to grind, 62
Angel, financial backer as, 61
Anne of Brittany, 127
Antony and Cleopatra, 25
Apollo, Greek god, 61
Appius and Virginia (Dennis), 121
Apple of his eye, 61
Apples, green, 143
April Fool's Day, 32-33
Architecture, Gothic, 134
The Art of Golfe (Simpson), 72
As the crow flies, 62
Athena, Greek goddess, 47
Awakening, sudden, of sleep-walker, 47-48

B

Babies, stork as bringer of, 47
Bacon, bringing home, 71
Bag
 holding the, 97
 in the, 97-98
Baker's dozen, 62
Balaclava, Battle of, 144
Bald eagle, as national symbol, 59

Balder, Scandinavian god, 37
Balls, golden, as sign for pawnbrokers, 50-51
Barber poles, 55
Barking up the wrong tree, 62-63
Barnstorming, 63
Baseball, origins, 145
Baseball bat, placement of trademark on, 85
Bats .300, 23-24
Beaverbrook, Lord, 69
Bed, getting up on the wrong side of, 43
Bedlam, 52
Beets, Harvard, 102
Behind the eight ball, 52
Bells, indicating time at sea by, 57
Bench mark, 144
Benedict, Samuel, 129
Berryman, Clifford, 57
Best foot forward, 64
Bible, Gideon, 55
The Big Apple, New York City as, 64
Big Ben, 18
Bitter end, 64
Blackball, 65
Black cat, and luck, 32
Blacklist, 65
Blessing, for sneezers, 53-54
Blood, blue, 65
Blow hot and cold, 67
Blue blood, of aristocrats, 65
Blue jeans, 67
Blue-sky laws, 68
Bobbies, London policemen as, 68
Bookworm, 68
Booth, John Wilkes, 82
Bootlegging, 68-69
Booz, E. S., 69
Booze, 69
Boston *Transcript,* 90
Bound feet, of Chinese women, 60
Boycott, Charles, 69
Boycotting, 69

Eye(s)
 evil, 48-49
 pull the wool over, 105

F

Face the music, 87
Fainting, during fall, 19
Fall, fainting or dying during, 19
Fans, sports enthusiasts as, 132
Fathers, surnames given to
 children, 21
Fat people, as jolly, 22
Fawkes, Guy, 94
A feather in his cap, 89
Feeling his oats, 90
Feet of Chinese women, bound,
 60
Fifteen, as tennis score term, 26
Fifth column, 13
Fingers, crossed, and luck, 41-42
Fire, out of the frying pan into,
 11-13
Firewood, cords of, 142-143
Fish
 as brain food, 14
 as Christian symbol, 57
Fisher, Samuel, 77
Fish in troubled waters, 21
Fists, as dukes, 129
Fits to a T, 13
Flag
 colors of, 53
 at half mast, as sign of
  mourning, 51
A flash in the pan, 89
Foot, twelve inches as, 67
Football field, as gridiron, 134
Fort Sill, Oklahoma, 43
Forty, as tennis score term, 26
Fort Yukon, Alaska, 17
Fourflusher, 142
Four hundred, 89
Four-leaf clover, and luck, 31
Fox, cunning of, 15
Franklin, Benjamin, 62, 147
Free-lancers, 127

French fries, 132
Freshmen, 132-133
Freud, Sigmund, as inventing
 term "id," 22-23
Freya, Scandinavian goddess, 37
Frostbite, rubbing with snow, 49
Frying pan, into fire from, 11-13
Funny bone, 133

G

Game, as tennis score term, 26
Gargantuan, 131
Gauntlet, run, 113
Gérôme, Jean Léon, 45
"Geronimo," paratrooper yell, 43
Get down to brass tacks, 90
Gets my goat, 96
Getting up on the wrong side of
 the bed, 43
Ghost writing, 133
Gideon Bible, 55
Gideon Society, 55-56
Gift horse, 107
Gifts for Christmas, Santa Claus
 as bringer of, 35
Goat, geting one's, 96
Godiva, Lady, 112
Go haywire, 91
Gold, all that glitters is not, 52
Golden balls, as sign for
 pawnbrokers, 50-51
Golf caddies, 73
Golf course
 as links, 72
 reason for eighteen holes on,
  30
Golfers, use of tees by, 30
Gone to pot, 91
A good break, 90
Gotham, New York City as,
 91-92
Gothic architecture, 134
"Go West, young man," and
 Greeley, 95
Graham, Sylvester, 134
Graham crackers, 134

About the Author:

Robert L. Shook's extensive business background includes being Chairman of the Board of American Executive Corporation and founder of the American Executive Life Insurance Company. He is now a full-time writer, with fourteen previous books to his credit, including *The Chief Executive Officers, The Shaklee Story, Winning Images, Successful Telephone Selling in the 80's,* and *Why Didn't I Think of That!* A graduate of Ohio State University, he resides in Columbus, Ohio. He has appeared on several hundred radio and television talk shows while on tour for various publishers.